I0756219

Praise for
Apology: Love as the State of Things

"We are all in receipt of divine gifts in the beginning and at the end. We are asked to be mindful of this in the middle. This worthy book goes to the heart of the matter in offering an existential witness and prophetic reminder of all of this in the gifts of divine love. It offers true testament to the weakness and poverty asked of us by Christ. It is witness in communicating with genuineness, lucidity, and steadfastness beyond the normal securities, and expressed with poetic touch and spiritual cadence. It is clued into the counterfeit doubles of Christianity, whether from the left or the right, and indeed in the middle. Very warmly recommended."—WILLIAM DESMOND, Cassiciacum Fellow, The Augustinian Institute, Villanova University, USA; Professor of Philosophy emeritus, Institute of Philosophy, KU Leuven, Belgium

"Whether one identifies with the Weak, the Compromised, or the Radicals—or perhaps some bricolage of these paradigms—readers will find in Stephen Bujno's *Apology* a provocation to contemplate subtle but deeply significant aspects of our world today. With echoes of Justin Martyr's first *Apology*, Bujno channels not only a similar attitude and keenness of insight, but a creative modification updated for our time. This is an immensely thought-provoking work, with a profound depth that is communicated in a very accessible style. I highly recommend *Apology* for anyone wanting a clearer vision of so much of what today has otherwise been obscured."—BRENDAN SAMMON, Associate Professor of Systematic and Historical Theology, Saint Joseph's University

"If 'traditionalism' means recovering the style, tone, and teaching of the early Fathers, this book is traditionalist. If 'radicalism' means getting to the 'roots' (*radix*) and applying them to the current moment, this book is radical. Only a 'radical traditionalism' can address the problems we face today—and Stephen Bujno addresses them in the same way St. Justin Martyr or St. Basil the Great did. A radicalism without tradition can only mean power without purpose; a tradition severed from its roots is a contradiction in terms."—JOHN MÉDAILLE, Instructor in Theology, University of Dallas

Apology: Love as the State of Things

APOLOGY

Love as the State of Things

⊕

Stephen Bujno

First published by Angelico Press 2026

For information, address:
Angelico Press
169 Monitor St.
Brooklyn, NY 11222
www.angelicopress.com

979-8-89280-180-5 (pbk)
979-8-89280-181-2 (cloth)
979-8-89280-182-9 (ebook)

Cover design: Michael Schrauzer

Table of Contents

Author's Preface

The unwelcome side effect of Christianity being tolerated is that one may live tolerably as a Christian. Little more is necessary to demonstrate that, than the disconnect between the received deposit of Christian faith and how many live as Christians. There is no shortage of books addressing that reality. This text, like others, proposes a response of personal reform, which then shapes one's witness to the secular age. But the spiritual transformation proposed in *Apology: Love as the State of Things* is not about private piety, personal resilience, or developing evangelical strategies. The goal is to make oneself weak. *Apology* offers, in narrative form, a response to the stealth of this spiritual threat. Apathy and indifference have compromised Christians of the developed world and dampened their faith-formed witness. Those twinned evils arise because the distinction between trust in Christ and seeking temporal security has become increasingly unclear. There is no enthusiasm for sacrifice without measurable gain, and without distinction between testimony and example, personal integrity—as a vague "authenticity"—becomes the measure of one's spirituality. So, to address the onset of apathy and indifference requires much more than catechetical correction or edifying encouragement. Therefore, this work intentionally mimics the style, tone, and syntax of Justin Martyr's AD 150 *Apology*. The reader should keep that in mind, as the style, tone, and syntax of this writing can appear awkward to contemporary eyes. The purpose of this imitation is that such a staging allows an argument for weakness to unfold that is neither didactic nor sermonizing. If the premise is that people listen more readily to witness than words, then truth embedded in the form of a narrative witness is more likely to reach those affected by apathy and indifference.

Two millennia separate inaugural Christianity from the present time. Though as a prayer answered, hostile adversaries of the Early Church have presently given way to Christians of the developed world living reasonably in peace. But as the identifiable oppression has waned, so too has the requisite courage and honor it engendered. Courage devolved into being true to oneself, and honor has been subsumed by careerism and titles. In the Early Church, those who remained faithful, moved by Christ's message of hope and mercy, were the seeds that exponentially expanded the Christian ranks. In an analogous way, like many entering the later span of their years, with the minority Christian sect now an accepted presence in the world, Christianity has reached middle age. Conformity to the world can easily be rationalized as the success of the Christian witness, with security as the hard-won prize. Admittedly, for many, physical threats remain, though not for the fortunate most. Like the young rich ruler, with his question of what is necessary for eternal life answered plainly, the proposal of weakness for Christ brings sorrow, and with it reform and witness withers. Today then, those pestilent vices do not arise from an authoritative government, nor do they simply result from the laity's disagreement with Church teachings, time-pressed schedules, liturgical boredom, or the dearth of convincing arguments.

If, in theory, most accept Paul's boast that power is made perfect in weakness, it is too readily dismissed as a charism for the few. It becomes easy to rationalize, pursuing only the minimum effort thought necessary for entry into everlasting life. That type of spiritual bargaining does not remain hidden to the world, and from it has arisen a distrust of what Christians profess, measured against how Christians in reality live. This project imagines the experienced cost of not living a truly authentic weakness. But perhaps more importantly, it illustrates the detrimental effect of presuming it to be a mere ideal. The world has witnessed Christians calculating spiritual risks against worldly status. That imbalance has led to a widespread lethargy and spiritual malaise. The prescribed solution of precarity is certainly difficult, and therefore because of that left untried. But precarity is not a destitute poverty. It rather is a voluntary insecurity that thrusts one into relational trust. Precarity, then, in tandem with hope to overcome apathy and mercy to temper indifference, comprises the internal response. With this realignment of word and deed, reform of self arises as the witness to the lived creed.

This *Apology* was my Lenten fast of 2023. The form of it as an idea, along with scribbled notes, had existed for many years. But I felt compelled to set aside the writing queue to bring this project to fruition. It was cathartic. Spiritual writings are very personal, and *Apology* was a response to my own spiritual apathy and indifference, and personal struggles with precarity. Too often, according to the Catholic hierarchy, moral scandal is measured by the adverse risk to reputation and property, rather than aberration from the moral life of the

Spirit. And too few live the poverty of Christ, let alone the voluntary poverty spoken of here. It is not unusual for bishops and priests sometimes to inhabit the mansions of past business magnates, or at least have access to lifestyles and vacations that remain beyond the grasp of the struggling working class. Many laity fare no better, demonstrating a similar disconnect. Catholic business owners and entrepreneurs can hardly be distinguished from any secular enterprise. Their prosperity is acclaimed as a blessing, and frequently sought as required revenue for parish renovations and school support. Any prelate who causes friction with a donor would likely be rebuffed by the local bishop for alienating their philanthropic assistance. What does this witness to, except that fundraising and financial stability, rather than precarity, are the accepted and necessary means to continue the work of Christ? And to a degree, it appears quite reasonable to seek insurance for future troubles, because charitable works are not free from expense. What is not certain, though, is how to apply Christ's admonition not to store up treasures that can be destroyed by moths and rust. And it is even less clear what deleterious effect such safeguarding might have as a witness to both the faithful and the world, who know too well that where one's treasure is, there too is their heart.

It is easy in light of all this to delve into apathy and indifference, and perhaps easier to place the blame on those who are thought to be Christian ministers and leaders, but fall short by example. But as my good wife Tina often says of the shortcomings of others, particularly the Catholic hierarchy and Christian leaders, one's faith is not in them, but in Christ. I, then, like many, struggle to find the balance between conviction and comfort, compassion and compromise. There is no simple spiritual metric determining when living in voluntary need becomes imprudent preparation. After all, Christ said that the birds of the air are fed without sowing or gathering, yet people die because they have not sowed or gathered. Nonetheless, I envision a Church that is voluntarily poor. A Church, living precariously, that has neither rich people to shmooze nor property to lose. I hope for a Church that is spiritually free to live as a witness in accordance with the faith revealed by the Incarnation. But at some sober point, in spiritual maturity, I must accept that *I am the Church.* Yet I, like all in the Church, am small and insignificant. Dorothy Day said that just because small individual steps seem insignificant, no one has the right to sit down and feel hopeless. There is much work to do. And may I add, it is Christ's work that is to be done.

So what follows is an account of hope and mercy, sustained by courage and honor, guarded by precarity. It is not intended to be a "what-if" version of history. But it does offer the possible conditions under which the weakness of Christ emerges as the only authentic witness to those inside and outside of Christ's formal Church. With no intent of world building, *Apology* envisions three basic faith expressions on the part of groups of people who boast an authentic pedigree with early Christianity. In the schema that follows, there are insufficient conditions necessarily present for what led to the onset and effects of the Reformation; therefore, Christianity as proposed here did not experience any denominational splintering. Therefore, the first are the Compromised, who alone represent Constantine's alliance between State and Church. The Compromised represent the hypocrisy found within the formal Church. The second group are the Radicals, who, though espousing the necessity of simple living and social justice, have tethered themselves to the academic sphere where the ideals of Christ have been severed from any source of grace. The efforts of the Radicals consist of social programs and community engagement, with little regard for revealed truth or personal transformation. Finally there are the Weak, the remnant of the Way who embrace precarity as an antidote to temporal power. They nurture the twin virtues of courage and honor, standing as a contradiction to the world, and thus irritating those in control. The Weak seek solely to be an icon of their Friend, a title they give to the Christ, who assured them they would no longer be known as servants if they did what was commanded of them. All of this is then rhetorically presented in the guise of a letter which one member of the Weak has penned to an unnamed ruler, in defense of the Way. As in the *Apology*, so it is in reality: when a Christian refuses to tolerate the secular ethos, the secular ethos will no longer tolerate Christianity. An added feature is a private devotion that I penned as a personal reflection, intended to be constructed physically, as a stepped journey on my own private property. It is called *The Way of the Weak*, which is replete with communal prayers, connecting Sacred Scripture to mercy and hope as the path to justice.

Preamble

When the Body fails to demonstrate missionary zeal, the spirit decays. In the decades since this testimony was quietly conveyed to us, we the Weak have only grown emboldened. More than two millennia ago Justin penned his *Apology*; and as it appears in the world to us now, both the form of apathy and fashion of reprisal has changed; but the same lack of hope and deterioration of courage that underlay the philosophers of his time has become manifest, in our days, in two deceptive variants. Therein lies the tragedy; each version claims continuity with our Friend. The Compromised, though ever congenial to the Weak in appearance, disclose their marginal pretense by a projected esteem and obedience, reducing hope to a merely worldly harmony and courage under the guise of doctrinal continuity; the Radical's faith, if one must call it that for public clarity, is plucked from a shrouded hope to provoke mystique by jargon, and courage stirred by empty maxims. Each proves more clever than the Weak's reproach. Then in reverence, as all are called to the Way, those who preach to the Eastern world, whereby distinct contrast between the visible and invisible is made plain, peril is expected; this was Justin's fate for his time in the West, which now renders the invisible but eclipsed by the visible. The General Secretary knows what yeast our hope and courage are, and tolerates us as benign to the State. But such false hope is spewed by the Compromised, as the Radicals trample what hope is given; equally carnal is the courage both think is expressed, respectively, by stalwart views, or acceptance of dismal realities.

Marginalizing the Way has led to inaction. Though Habermas was resolved to offer action, figures of this kind failed to consider that the absence of form leaves any remaining matter lifeless. The converse is no less pernicious, as maintaining form without proper matter adorns its insipid taste with worldly spoils. Each, discarding the garb of precarity's protection of discomfort, has, with it, jettisoned hope and courage; each, with indifference or disbelief, has merited Therèse's admonition, that by spurning such love and confidence, the soul has become fearful of so affectionate a Friend, who alone is to be singularly loved. Thus, the Secretary gladly confirms the Compromised, whose doctrine prospers only the unbelief of believers, and wills a State to accept as a creed the curtain of indifference which Radicals boast as mind-dependent remedies. So there we have it, friends of our Friend: where one facet has proven their infidelity to weakness, our Friend has granted the Compromised the earthly power for which they earnestly pleaded. And as for the other facet, whose suspicion of inherited truths has been distilled to only one comprehensible persuasion: the Radicals' power has been granted, but under the guise of reason. Then each, by its charm, has robbed the believers of a faith deposited in full; as in their home, with doors locked but windows open wide the thieves' gate, their anti-liturgy does violence only to the Kingdom of Heaven. With each tenet proposed, souls no longer die for a faith, but rather die in their faithlessness, either melded to earthly powers, or solace found by adaptation to present comforts.

This testimony, shared with you again on the anniversary of our Weak's departure to the East and the testimony gained for us, lays bare by what form the Compromised lack humility and those so-called Radicals forfeit joy. Each dissolve hope and mercy, and thus the harvest of justice. But since the inactivity of neither impostor threatens State interests, both are left to the preoccupation with the other. Justin was convicted of subversion; perceived rebellion warrants harsh treatment for sedition. Such a threat remains for the Weak, and has prompted welcomed ire. What differs from the reign of Antoninus is only the identity of the gods to whom worship is thought due. The relic of each remains; what threatens progress, threatens power. What was given to those He loves, now apportioned to the Weak by our Friend, thus threatens progress. Yet what was given but to welcome the stranger into one's home; to give comfort to the elderly; for us to marry and bear children by the womb; determined not to kill the unborn; to wipe out divisions; not to select offspring by desired traits and societal values; above all, to live in precarity; to seek needs and not wants; and, finally, to give one's physical life rather than surrender these good things. Such simple truths simply threaten power. Yet these things are the truth, my fellow Weak; these are such that have been given to us. So then, as Justin admonished us in his *Apology*, let us exercise such wisdom in our own time; let this *Apology* continue to suffice. No one who is rightly minded turns from true belief to false hope; be not discouraged; fall not into unbelief; in authentic courage, repel indifference and gain hope. Then may your spirit live and zeal advance.

I
Address

My fate is known. I will not cheat death, but I have endeavored to strike a bargain as to the present state of things, which I will now address. As to the merits of this undertaking, it is quite hidden from me to what extent it will be an advantage for followers of our Friend who are also on pilgrimage. That lies solely with you, my esteemed General Secretary; for myself, I am quite content and satisfied to the fullest that you have asked of me, who am removed from loved ones and reserved for purposes quite hidden, personally to make clear the wellspring of mercy I seek and the hope I retain.

I do reflect upon how you have come to choose such an inadequate ambassador; to my mind, I am an unlikely choice. That is not intended as a critique of your certitude, but the notion still tests the limits of my capacity. Nonetheless, in what follows I will indulge your well-known penchant for dichotomy and riddled speech, for the clarity you think they unveil and the thrill of uncovering logical absurdities. Your intelligence is renowned; may peace from the contrasts and comparisons I provide grant concord between us. I then will speak, in this letter, not in the way in which I would desire to express the truth, as it has been handed down to us; but rather in the manner and tone by which it must be heard. Though there is something of evident prominence in you—that powers greater than you or I have elected to bear this record of witness of the Weak to you—I, on my part, seek to be convinced by my own words, and, as they reach your eyes and ears, may a semblance of trust be found. Your learned status is celebrated; may my words reach that height! My hesitation, my anxiety, wagers that such finesse as I offer in concealed expression will be found wanting.

II

The Obligation of Justice

We implore all who seek what is true and pious, clamor not with arbitrary bickering. Distinguish the opinion of a fool from the wanderings of a learned philosophical mind. In both cases, there is seemingly a narrative which cannot be shared, nor should either be distributed. Nor does it attain veracity merely by a willingness to lay down one's life, as then both patriots and the pious would share the company of zealots. I, therefore, have no intention of playing into your favor by either the use of word or wit; I would think it patronizing and you would rightly hold such a perspective in contempt. That said, those of us who have stayed in the race wait to see it accomplished; reputation can be ruined in the public sphere, and circumstances more severe have and will continue to be levied against us. But with love for life and family, equal to all, such powers laid at your feet dissolve not with our deaths, but the demise of our spirits; which belong to neither of us, nor, in light of that, is there any Earthly power which can destroy them.

III
The Form of My Efforts

For quite some time we, the Weak, have become accustomed to our defenses finding no resolve. The propaganda outlets of media brands and inflaming text have barred us from a just hearing. Just as with older means of delivering such content socially, the mindless feed on headlines, consistent with their preferences. You have nonetheless sought such a seminal approach, where what is offered arrives at your mind unfiltered; I intend to offer just that. In that regard many of our lot have cautioned me from such an approach; for the conditions are that we should voluntarily commit to your justice, and that is no slight wager on our part, that, from our perspective, justice will prevail. But I welcome the higher party's trap, as that risk is the lower party's opportunity: it is that which both garners our hope and increases fear in those of us who find no other recourse but to courageously offer you our case. For that vulnerability you would demand, be it given with no opposition, nor resisted by weapon or by defenses. I still pray that you will allow the clear path of certainty, as the Philosopher has held, to be the standard of your justice and not popular hostility, which is in such abundance, and would, without compromise, find resounding applause against us if you choose to support our continued ridicule and repression. This offer, which is actually a response, is that in this circumstance, one will be heard; the wise will listen, and both will be vindicated. What will be given herein is complete, and the form of it rational; with no appeal to dogma outside your domain. If I fall short in this, then let me alone be judged incompetent, and the futility of this effort remain not in what is proposed, but in the weakness of the one who proposes.

IV

The Form of Our Contrariness

It is acknowledged that weakness is not a virtue to those who desire influence, predicating it on power. So to recognize one as Weak, in our precarity, places each of us, the faithful, in a deliberately insecure predicament. Those who are sick themselves, cannot treat the malady: if our pecuniary disadvantage is self-imposed, let others be our physician, and, further, let their insults fill our prescription. This is accepted, and in fact becomes the boast of the Weak. If there are found those counted among us who disparage courage and honor—those two great virtues languishing in these times—and if, by omission, they have occasioned injustices, then let their offense reside with them alone. Weakness without willingness is indeed pitiable; our piety prefers to preserve the converse. Let the fragile withdraw, from ours, the identity they spoil, and rather keep to their own kind, so that the distance between them and us should be clear. Yet, alas, the balanced ideal is granted to no known group; therefore allow, I pray, this testimony to attest to those who earnestly strive to remain firm, and, by allowing our weakness to become the means of resistance, such deficiency or extreme I argue now before you.

If, on account of those who fall short even by this measure, those whom society belittles and chastises with both barbs and blows, then, by association with them, allow us all to suffer on their behalf. This is acceptable. But if their chastisement is meted out not because of their professed faith, but accidentally, because of flaws in character that all possess, then do what you will within justice, and remove the taint of their hopelessness; for it is their own. But I humbly submit that too often, the authorities and influencers have not refrained from hasty generalizations, having not only accused, but punished those who stand as variants to culture and State. Likewise, the elect has suffered these same contortions of truth by you to whom I now appeal; how many of our patriarchs have been derided in death, yet you and the many maintain such certainty, as though any present cultural heroes could withstand future scrutiny of equal measure. The moral virtuosos have retrospectively emended a pithy aphorism—"time heals all wounds"—to suggest that time *worsens* all wounds, forgetting how the thin air they breathe at such moral heights affects not just mood, but cognition. The logic of my demand, then, is that if any of the Weak, who indeed stand by the creed of life and tongue, are accused because they hold what the Absolute has revealed through our Friend; then nothing but allowing their own testimony to confer on them the veracity of your claims of cultural impiety remains. Let them be questioned, allow the circulators of mistruth and puffers to accept discovery: the heterodox of culture and academia accept such a discipline, which, in reality, is a crown. But if they become vague in their defense, or tenuous in the course of explaining, though you are right to inquire further into the sum of what they profess, let the manner in which they assume to be orthodox by your principled standard be the balance of judgment and acquittal.

Our piety, as understood and adopted by the Weak, is rationally accepted as impiety from your perspective;

but to us, such lack of conviction on the part of those who inform you incorrectly of our mistaken misdeeds, otherwise appears to be wicked and cowardly from our perspective, and thus rationally confirms to us that we are indeed pious. All sects who follow our Friend are not without common bond, but neither are we so formally attached that the Authority which one enjoys extends to all; we are confined to the same genus, with deviations, slight not severe, based on differing charism, form, and station. But please hear me; there are those among you who receive accolades for their cleverness; which, gained at our expense, even if officially discouraged, is nonetheless granted allowance, and only reined in when the incident or conflation conflicts with the functioning of the State. If disunity foils your attempts at disuniting us, and this is your frustration, the unity that your State enjoys leaves no place where our reproach could easily find its mark; but an inability to diminish persecution becomes our frustration.

V

It is the Truth Which is Contested

For this reason, you say we hate the State; and are against the truths you admire. But I assure you that we hold much which you would arguably regard as universal. The highest of those things are claimed by our nature, if only implicitly known. Yet it is by such means that we claim to ascertain those proper ends; consider such by contrast towards the ends of the kingdom you secure and the ends of the Kingdom for which we endure.

It is in that way which we, I say the Weak, are falsely accused of being indifferent to the pursuit of the good things commonly shared, empiricism and power among them, but without the latter distorting the former. Why then, we ask, have the reasons not been plainly requested for your account? So many of the tenets of this, our contemporary time, are accepted with little justification; and, to our mind, these tenets are easily exposed ideologies. Not only has the nature of beings been discarded, but constructed human interests have been promulgated as god-certain dictates. Was not the Philosopher pilloried for exposing the five wounds of the subjected followers of our Friend? How much more than He with outstretched hands are you exposed!

Accused of fostering aberrations, the Philosopher accepted censure with humility. I do not temper such compliance, holding it as my fault; nor do I refuse to suffer fools. These deficits of partial truths accepted, form a vacuum, imploring the powerful who desire to remain so, to act as State advocates, and achieving nothing but to make them the beneficiaries of prestige. If our Friend was the visible Icon of divinity among creation, then those who usurp His trust are idols of humanity among the divine; they remain strong only to the impious, not to us, who remain His pious Weak. To these individuals there can be no comparison with such authentic truths, that, being eternal, are shared between your greatness and what we, the Weak, endeavor to hold firm. As there is a single truth, empiricism does not distort reality; in the words of Augustine, no man is made unhappy by knowledge; but once deconstructed, they align inductive ideas with forged mistruths that both the Weak, and we pray, the State, hold in disdain. Our Friend, as true image, cannot be reduced to man for others, where idol becomes icon; whereas our Friend as true image, Man for self, preserved for others, as icon, becomes the Ideal. I am speaking here of truth allied with man's Being; this is the idea of Love that I offer you.

VI

Our Impurity is Tied to Falsehood

But you have charged us with deviation from the truth as the propagandists have handed it to you, and if by truth one means assent to the inventions of power and its means, regarding our Friend as a mere man, and thinking of matter as the sole lens of truth, then we hold these ideas to be degenerate. It is to those who defer to unmediated reason in tandem with Revealed truth that we hold our Friend, the revealer of truth, as the Absolute; who alone contains all genuine forms, mediated by the irresistible force of Love that consumes all peoples. The impurity you hold us to issues only from this single, three-fold source; and therefore if that be the charge, then designate us impure.

VII

Some Claim Weakness as Individual Actors

All understand that the State has seized many, and ostracized countless others for their lack of adherence to adopted norms. You accuse us of dislodging your authority, but it is the eternal truths that we beseech you first to consider; the greatest of us, handed to the least in us. For the Weak pose no threat to you, and we further beseech you that, secondly, you consider the extent to which our firmness is an advantage to you, in both its clarity and consistency. The Compromised have property and wealth, and, from those elements, possess control; the Radicals, diluted and erratic, have pretense and ascendancy and, from those, possess leadership; and both, though they publicly affirm the State's utterances, and thus appear to you to be wise, speak only with sophistic tongues, and, by a charade-like stance, make their appeal. But for our part, any among the Weak who do not do what you desire, unless it too is unjust in accordance with our Friend, then Great One, condemn them; silence them as you may. But do so on account of their own apparent maturations and not by their heritage, and thus a perceived affiliation with the Weak. If they resist subjective truths based on societal interests, then count them among us. But if those truths are shown to be ironically opposed to the State's interests and the Weak's pledges, then acquit us of that stance, for we too find such to be only farcical guardians of joyless truths. Even those whom we do count among our immediate fold, yet fall short of our ideals, need no correction, for such diluted affiliations as they have with the Compromised and Radicals are indelible marks on their character, and by that alone will punishment be meted out until eternal Love intercedes.

VIII

The Weak Seek the Mean

We are, with easy discourse, capable of conforming to the semblance of cooperation with the culture you espouse, to the extent that justice found in the pursuit of work and food, with the freedom to address our truth, is present in us, and by that you will find us compliant. Yet falsehood is contrary to being Weak. Anticipating that all things will be brought into the light, even though nothing can resist Love's call, we seek to be like our Friend and stand witness to eternal truths. How can we then turn from the One who, instructing those we call past sisters and brothers of the Weak, unite with a spirit that conforms to any particular age? This is why we make little distinction between the unknown Compromised and the self-declared Radicals. They are errors of excess and deficiency, and the Weak seek the mean. If this, by your reckoning, either seems futile and, for that reason, disadvantageous; or if, simply because it is not empirically verifiable, it is thought to be a feeble endeavor; then by those accounts, convict us. They who are Compromised allow their prosperity to conceal the rot; and those thought to be Radicals have twisted reason to fit their ideology; the former emphasize what is deemed worth living for, and the latter offer nothing of substance to die for. We, the Weak, admit to not seeking the advantages laid out by gain; for from that only power erupts. Likewise, we, the Weak, will not deconstruct our Friend to fit the academy, and, by that, do what appears digestible to the learned. We, the Weak, prefer to propagate only that which has been handed down to us; its untimeliness to present prosperity and ideology is of no concern; rather than conferred by needs or calculations among the so-called wise, our wisdom seeks neither cleverness for gain nor reputation obtained.

IX

The Ignorant Fool Seeks the Corruptible

The very hope for us then lies in that which is low until we the Weak, by Love, are made high. For the Compromised, the accomplishments of wealth offer no shield against happiness when this age passes. They heed not what was demanded of the Rich Ruler, and are willing to give all they have only after death; as an act of altruistic narcissism, it is only at their physical demise that finally, without defense, in full paradox, that becomes the single instance in respect of which they choose to admit their weakness. For the Radicals, what can be handed down—though it is in fact imposed—except loosely tied maxims, seasoned and borrowed wit? They worship a headless god, with their fragility begging admiration from the grave by the legacy of letters that future intellectuals will espouse as brilliance by affiliation with the obtuse. You see that many, then, count themselves of our heritage; sadly, we the Weak have no trademark on the Way; but by forged simulation elevating their proud status, others find solace in such comforts as I have stated. This leaves them, in our eyes, as soulless beings, carcasses of malevolence. The Compromised assemble in deified castles, and create monuments of ornamental testament to our Friend; but in so doing, they place their hope in carved stone and gilded plaster, raiment, apparel, stations of honor, with rubrics scripted for ostentation; and thus they have fashioned only flamboyant insults to the Absolute, whom they have elevated as an ornament. The Radicals who have grafted themselves on to our heritage; find comfort in their pretension, guffawing at those who are thought incapable of comprehending the depth of their lurid speech; such a veneer of tortuous serpentine discourse functions merely as coded in-speak, making a god in their image. Twinned evils: this is but the pompous Compromised's embellishment added to the Radical's ornamental, embroidered text and speech; the non-difference of both is a sinister plot to locate the Infinite in the finite. It is true that the Infinite is revealed in the finite, but I put it to you that the converse is an insult to intelligence, and stands as an offense to the Absolute.

You, dear Secretary, at least consistent in not affirming the deity you deny, do not escape rational castigation. When Tyson asked what reaction Hitchens would offer if the Absolute were found to be true after death, Hitchens replied that he would ask, why not more proof of this God now? I tell you that the Absolute, appealing to his mathematical mind, would ask him how it could be thought that the Infinite could possibly be contained within the finite. How unlike, in consequence, are the Compromised and the Radicals; who express the Infinite as only finite, and, in that finiteness, attempt to compress the Infinite. Not only can the Infinite not be contained by the finite, which the unbelieving empiricists seem to reject, but the corruptible will not elicit the incorruptible, as those of our erroneous heritage assume. In a Socratic approach, the soul has an affinity with the eternal, and thus, unlike the body, does not perish, so it deserves the highest interest. We assert that vice is more attached to the material and the corruptible, but we neither discard nor elevate that which holds our form; both remain, for us, as the person. But the Weak do not work to preserve the temporary aspects of being when eternity does not inherit such investment, nor do they think that the eternal city must be perfectly reflected in the temporal city. The caretakers of the Compromised, which the State enjoins, set themselves up as custodians of all, but we share only ancestry with them. Their power, which ensues and props them up, is undone by the Weak's hope in prioritizing the incorruptible form, which stands apart from the present age. And sharing Socrates's impiety, and the righteousness of the Old Covenant, over the Compromised and Radicals, we choose that which pleases the Absolute, remaining unshielded against their stones of platitudinous prose; the Weak, having courage and retaining honor, willingly drink the hemlock given by society and its agents.

X

The Absolute is Known in Conscience by Law

Those virtues, then, which flow in perfection solely from the Absolute, and barely reflect the fulfillment of all beauty, truth, and goodness, remain discoverable in each nature that you regrettably reject. They are found by us to be immutable, preservable, and thus excellent. From the breath of the Creator all forms become particular; brought into existence in love, they issue forth from the heart of the Absolute, who made Himself known to us in fullness upon entering creation. Not from any happy fault did this Incarnate Friend enter our likeness, but from the beginning this Being, unlike all others, willed by His own power that He become low so that we might become high. In the present, we, like Him, remain low, manifesting our suffering and corruption, and accept, as the Philosopher has said, our embeddedness with the Eternal in such an Idea as an appurtenance. That Idea, residing in each of His then elevated creation, presents for the Creator refuge, where reason and will may align with the Logos, from which time has sprung as origin. Therefore, no pattern writ by the created can be affected, except it align with the Eternal design. It is where, as conscience, the Idea expressed by this pattern guides creation. Those that ally with creation, separated from this locution of conscience, are entangled, proud and conceited, in vice; and by that they profane the sublime, and, in the case before you, deride us, the Weak; any appearance of communion is but a thin shell.

XI

The Weak Seek Only the Incorruptible

Only with that reckoning confirmed, our plan is made clear; such desired weakness is fodder to the powerful and those seekers of prestige. Our precarity finds riches to be carnal prudence under the guise of planning and preservation, and to perversely invert the claim of our Friend, who sought neither position nor revolution while among us, those many centuries now past. Ample goods are foolish to us; you claim this weakness may be our demise, and so it is true. But our present weakness should not be mistakenly thought of as a permanent state; it is a means to an end, one that, when this momentary condition has passed, will demonstrate itself as a strength that, in the here and now, cannot be confirmed, save by our testimony of faith and equal willingness to remain temperately in want, while in this unjust world, while the next is not yet visible.

XII

Flattery and Prestige are Meaningless

How is it held then that the Absolute, who is outside of time, could not effortlessly identify as committed or omitted any action or thought in time? Every eon is an instant; all time, collectively, is but an eternal now. It is a participatory anamnesis. For us it is precisely in the quality of our acts that each individual is rendered justice, predicated on His mercy and hope in us; the purification that awaits everyone would be avoided at all costs; except that many do not keep this very fact close to their mind or heart. With no disrespect, Secretary, your eyes and ears are ubiquitous in the State, and yet many of your citizens escape detection when abdicating your demands. How different it would be if, in full and convincing knowledge, no consequence existed for any thoughts they share, which lead to acts contrary to your laws! There would be no restraint without your demanded justice; immunity would be antecedent; what role of hope, and recompense nullified; illicitness undetected requires no mercy, yet we require it in full.

For the Weak, this is why our hope, here and now, is placed with precarity; it alone has the ability to reduce thirst for power and control, and counter the error of relegating the empirical to the material. We need not be so carefully monitored when our voluntary situation confines contrary urges. You admit this to be so; but counter that it is in this life that one is to be judged, and that the very thing we detest, power and intellectual pride, you count as fortune to have in excess and on full display. In your scheme, then, by shedding your power, you grant mercy; and many conjure hope by trusting in that mercy. We, the Weak, see the similitude between you and those who claim our heredity; those god-building Radicals as a body worship the headless Christ; and the god-idolizing Compromised have found it expedient for the body to worship the Christless head. Your version of scientific socialism is no different in practice from the Compromised's therapeutic deism or the Radical's therapeutic socialism. Therefore I urge you to consider, for those of us who respectfully know otherwise, what nonexistent threat in reality we are to you, even in the distance of value we share from your established governance. You issue forth laws, so that the polis knows that you are sincere in your decree. Because it is certain that some individuals must be breaking those laws, the Weak become easy prey to demonstrate your strict justice and stand as warning in proxy to others; each public example of your justice on us is meant to stand as the perceived consequent for the many and a deterrent, thus soliciting calls for mercy which you think as inverse proportion to your justice.

The Compromised and Radicals, both so weak in character, follow what is visibly common between them and you, but only so as to curry favor, though when not under your watchful eye, they think and do the opposite. They are cunning and we are naïve; yet even in our naivety we stay true to that which is common, even if veiled from you who deny the natures to which we rightly conform our judgments. They only appear to follow the decree by letter, yet in truth we do so in spirit, a spirit whose nature you have not yet accounted for. They avoid your detection by dereliction; we thrust forward our virtues publicly, and are denounced for our disclosure. We, the Weak, do so in holy fear of the Absolute from whom nothing is hidden; the Compromised and Radicals do so fearing power abatement or psychological marginalization, relative to your great position. From you, by comparison to the Absolute, much can be hidden, and from them correspondingly, much can be taken. What I say to you is that we contain our thoughts and actions to align with our nature, and it is the same nature that you share with us, thus we are just like you and hold and announce it with our lives. It is sensible, then, to maintain that in truth; our thoughts and actions align with your better angels; we ask that you discern them.

We contend that all sensible individuals would choose this path, if it was given a fair hearing in the public square; and by further ironic stance, on our part, this reversal of justice which we suffer is both welcomed and expected. It has been proclaimed to us in the memoirs of the Apostles to anticipate such derision, given not as a future-telling, but simply as the foreseen application of truth in line with one's nature, contrasted with the understanding that according to the world, the Compromised access advantage, and the Radicals pursue prestige—as if the Absolute were ignorant, and you Secretary, were absolute. The Compromised flatter others for advance; the Radicals flatter themselves for attention. To the extent that this can be made plainly known, then to that measure will ignorance alone of what one's nature calls each to do fail to extinguish falsity. We aim to satisfy the eternal, not the temporal.

XIII

By Reason We Uphold the Author of Reason

I beseech you, then, to accept that it is not we who should be set out as an example of justice, for you to retain control over those who do not do what we do willingly. We adhere to the nature given to us; to which we are inclined not only for the sake of our sustenance, but as a celebration of humanity, as the pinnacle of creation who are in genuine need, in accord with our nature. We do not impose our precarity on others but merely propose it. Further, unlike the materialists, we require so little materially, and, by doing so, preserve the creation from exploitation; whereas those who seek worldly gain and societal change have depleted resources which they themselves claim to be irreplaceable. Their dwellings are spacious, heating the exterior for entertainment, and unreasonably cooling the interior for comfort; they travel liberally, purchasing carbon emissions from the poor to expand their luxury. Do you not think this ironic, that those who are not of the world care most for this world, and live most in accordance with such terrestrial philanthropy, so as to preserve the needs of those who admit that they are of the world, and who should prioritize its habitable condition, while the latter deplete resources of all who are in the world? What we do is done as a tribute to our Creator; and our action, though here in reality an inaction, is offered as an environmental canticle, an integral ecology.

You know our story, and what formed us: that He who calls us friends, once entered, did redeem a world, and, for this great act, was set upon a tree, a scapegoat to bear the injustice that His presence revealed. Such is our lot now. The world's hymn was His demise; and only after piercing His side did Longinus confess what others knew by faith. But rather this event for us has become an icon; the Man who was disfigured by the world, became the means to transfigure the world; and the uncreated Creator who entered created creation, became a sign of contradiction to the world, of which from His very thoughts a sign was issued. Our Friend now has set us, His Weak, to be icons of the Uncreated to the created, in this already but not yet world; and before you, we now stand as a contradiction. This is His mystery, hidden in our Way; take heed.

XIV

The Compromised and Radicals Have Gone Astray

Little I have to offer, yet I will further call your attention to the deceit of others which I have spoken of, and whom you conflate with us, the Weak. Wormwood was cautioned to keep the patient alive through middle age, so that, sensing themselves as part of the world, only then will an individual lower their guard, and the world will become a part of them. So what is our habit? The mystery we keep hidden is on full display for those who have gratuitously knitted themselves to the world, and the dominion of the world is grateful for their effort; and by their error, they only magnify our certainty. The Great Liar is just that, a Liar, one without match. Whenever the bluff is uncovered, know that it is but a diversion, a stone thrown in the bush to solicit attention away from the culprit in shadowy refuge. The Weak knit not to the world; that which is good for the person cannot be outside of Eternal truth.

Many weigh the goods, and from that balance, calculate which thought or action such an ethic prescribes, and how it might be interpreted as such. But the full consequences remain aloof and will not appear while reparable. The first child born of the petri dish did not immediately point to endless cryopreserved embryos, and those snowflakes did not consequentially suggest that there would soon follow male cells, regained with potential to form an ovum. What of this then? We remind the Compromised that the cincture is not an organic growth of purity, and that the stole does not confer power. Those then of the Radicals who adhere to the non-real, and boast of the Nietzschean requiem, think they found death in a body where there is only sickness; and in that master's claim they, by a fluke of design, assume the posture of the herd they think to shepherd. We, the Weak, are despised, yet not less than our Friend was despised. Neither counterfeit body has detected the obvious, that the world's love is the mark of falsehood; and, as Paul warned, the State will arise as corrected agents of wrath when found out. We hold out, yet that may be your unwitting response.

The propaganda from each has turned the veracity of truth into a measure of outrage by you, and the cultured peerage. Authenticity then becomes appearance, and beauty mere titillation; but our prayer remains, both with you and for them, that all hearts will turn toward this Idea given to all, as a synderesis of love. We say to cast off then all forms of prestige: take no wealth, save that which is necessary for dignified living. Remain with the one to whom you have committed yourself; the Covenant is binding. Seek no remission of sin outside of the spring of Love. Our Friend spoke with simple words; and even if His words were veiled, they were granted safe keeping to a community of those whose story, now unveiled, has become ours. In the beginning, our Friend was the Logos, says John, and from this Logos His creativity issued forth. His lot was our lot through Constantine, who, by our reckoning, is a synonym for compromise. Embracing an advantageous faith, it eased persecution for some, while for other expressions it only increased. Julian easily ferreted out the bidirectional swaying of truth, that found solace in neither the Way nor the Forms. He buried his uncle; in

Chalcedon we took our stand. Adapting by gradations, the Compromised to this day bears that mark; and we—for it was only later in Persia—were spared by hospitality of grace and the patronage of fate.

Today, as then, Secretary, the Absolute will use those whom some men have hailed above other men, for purposes unforeseen in their calculations, and contrary to desired ends. The Council of Germania unmasks the industrialization that spewed forth its errors. The land retained such paganism and heresies, as the Compromised never expanded beyond the cults of avarice who sought favor in worldly leaders; let it be obvious then, why today, the Compromised finds such affinity for the comfort which progress has given. And, in like condition, why the Radicals seek only to establish the same goals, via distinct means; they took the principle of Engels's knight-errant on self-worth and identity, and pushed for Hegel's ethical life, to find only in reason its promise in the present. Neither the Compromised nor the Radicals, in one unholy irony, recognize that their distance from each other is in theory but not practice. As with globalization, opposed by each political pole, where the progressives sought to contain capital expansion, the conservatives sought to contain cultural erosion; this was misplaced thinking, since to be in front of the truth is no less dim-witted than impeding progression. Precarity, now as then, foils the bait; alone staves off such syncretic union and maintains the principled Weak, who hold not a centrist view. The Way does not navigate between wandering rocks and the siren's lure as their position, but by so doing, avoids the fate each would bring, and steadies the course with Ithaca in mind.

XV

How and Why the Weak Remain True

It is the same reason by which I, Stephen, now implore you to elevate what He has given me, and most have in greater abundance; I speak of reason, so that it may become the gate to desires and be now brought fully to bear on this point. Consider the covenant and creation powers devoted to it. We have not spoiled the sign; it has become obscured from the world, and we are held in contempt as cultivators of intolerance. Who else among our people retains the union which is to mirror our Friend's coupling with creation, an icon of our Friend's gift to the Absolute? Think slowly, Secretary; reduced to consensual, contractual expressions of sexual desire, what essence exists which would cease to discriminate? None, and none were offered; worse yet, none are thought possible, so that, without essence, the institution rationally dissolves. Where propagation came to represent the union *in toto* and love as accidental, love became essential, and propagation superfluous: conjugality was heralded as a self-defeating norm, but no alternative norm was proffered, save that of preference. Where there is preference, the libido has become a consumer's notion ratified by satisfaction; one's desire enters the metric, and, both undirected by reason and unchecked by Law, such urges press friendships into expressions lacking permanence and exclusivity, automatons employed to salvage loneliness. Such continuum logic was mocked as fallacious; yet the polis, driven mad, was never instructed in the chain of causal reasoning which was thought to render our reproach invalid. The Weak asked, "What is it?" and were told that only when meaning has no demarcation can inequity result; but this was but the asphyxiation of significance.

What has just been proffered by me, is by Gessen, whose work you have read, so much more poignantly articulated; for when supplied by an advocate, such correction from a shared identity does not so easily trigger violation, and is found less distasteful to the palate. Then, with reproduction as the emblem of technology, the chasm widened, replete with depersonalizing methods, indispensable for sustaining our kind. You, Great Secretary, know at first hand the market-driven manufacturing of life, the dependency on exowombs and what results from it, the reprogramming of pluripotent cells for calculated results from summoning nature. This mastery of nature, said Lewis, was only to be complete when the mastery of human nature itself could be overcome, the last bit of freedom to drown in the sea of progress; and with that, technology and economy perfectly meshed. From this *reductio* arose the logical evolution of thought, when science gained the capacity of sex-shifting: genetic expressions became clinically malleable, susceptible of being redetermined so that, therapeutically, what once was possible only accidentally, became essentially possible—coupled with the irony that gender became necessarily binary, in order to accommodate the visible expression of the genetic shift, the permutation required a bilateral phenotype for positive detection. Otherwise, what market is there for a costly therapy that does not bear a noticeable gain, or as in this case, a recognizable reversal? With no sovereign borders, meaning fell to pockets of power for the sake of control by influential designers; honor and courage were vacated from the calculated result which neither could nurture except by perversion causing degradation and diffidence. Then the value of diversity promised the spectrum, as a secondary benefit, to be the harbinger of fairness; the Weak, however, argued that distinction alone cultivates respect, thus establishing solidarity. Where they found dualism in variety, we maintained fluidity in the determined. So, those of the world have gained their treasure, but for all it has profited them, what has been given in exchange; except the denial of a nature which is a treasure, present as the Idea of love? Yet nothing is outside of the Absolute's purview; this has already been said.

But here, know that nothing lies beyond His hope. As fair Portia pleaded that the quality of mercy be not strained, for from Heaven it drops on all as gentle rain, so we must turn away from Shylock's plot. Although justice was not done to him, it was wished that turpitude should be returned to the source from which it came. But we affirm this nature, so, in your heart now, as a nature, Secretary, in which, by mercy, you will be twice blessed; it is an attribute of the Absolute no less given as gentle rain to you than, by your portion, it may now fall on us, and myself. Then I ask of you, allow your mind to embrace the immutable: censure not these words of mine, lest you confront them with logic which would demonstrate their demise. If what I argue is sound, with your heart seek only the incorruptible, and nullify not my reasoning. The Absolute, again, who both knows and sees what no man can know or see, will offer a return no earthly power or prestige can confer.

Peace will issue from your presence, and from that peace flows justice. The former always precedes the latter, and when the latter is found, there too is the former. Seek that, not justice first, which disrupts peace; then, by possessing and dispensing both, greatness will be your honor.

XVI

Punish Those Who Follow Our Friend in Name Only

The Weak espouse the virtues of honor and courage. Where honor solicits excellence, courage counters the irascible; to those ends we are compelled by patience that strives for justice, and gentleness which endeavors to steel against affliction. This, then, is the intent of our will. You see how honor is tied to excellence; like Aurelias, we find that if something is appropriate for man, then we can assume that it must also be within reach, for in this the virtue of honor is crowned by hope. Likewise then, courage implies the notion of a power under control, and, like a horse that submits to reins, for the sake of our Friend, and like our Friend, we temper provocation, which inaugurates the virtue of mercy. The consummation of such honor and mercy engenders justice. So, for you who are in search of justice, do not let your restlessness and cruelty serve as the greater members among you.

Let the antithesis be your word; in and by that, you will unwittingly serve our Friend, who alone is good and the Creator of all things visible and invisible. For our part, we eat what is necessary; consume in habit that which sustains our dignity; seek nothing which adorns the body and sets us apart from the lowest among us. This is how you will first know who among us is driven by Love's power. Let the light of the sun expose truth and error, as the Absolute in glory reveals the deeds of all. It is not by plea alone which compels the Idea of being to align with the Absolute Being, but such faith is borne out as beaten and despised. Therefore, do not hold to account on our behalf those who imitate anything which strays from the Way. It is within your power to punish those who retain the name of our Friend, but do not follow Him as I have laid out; as such, it is within your power to be severe to us. Such forfeiters yield to the urge; and, to validate their shortcomings, ratify their frailty by adopting such impuissance; it is, in short, an ethic of concession. In any punishment you levy upon spurious actors, our hopes will proportionally increase. But a caution to you: recall that patience and gentleness are not shortcomings, but benchmarks of honor and courage. Be just.

XVII

Our Disobedience is Only To Falsehood

Here I will ask directly; Secretary, if you can report one instance where those that we count among us have not offered to the State what is due; you see how highly we revere justice. This is again why I am perplexed; our Friend was driven to Golgotha not for civil disobedience, but for being despised by those to whom His words brought conviction. He had the power, with one glance towards Eternity, or an affirming nod to a host of Angelic defenders, to annihilate all enemies; but this should only serve to make His incorruptible nature known. Such a vulgar display of power would only mute created man's free agency. Know this, then: this is why we would never rise up ourselves, for we do not proportionately render back that which was given; but rather withhold injustice when injustice is served. So, be a wise judge, and be aware that we offer no civil disobedience to you. For as He has emptied Himself for all creation, we empty ourselves for all He created. The Absolute requires little of those who do not bear His seal, but all from those He has confirmed; and from those where all is asked by the Absolute, we strive to give all to those whom the Absolute loves, which are all. So, then, to follow such logic, from you we take nothing, but in splendid hope, give all, so that such emptiness, if not from you, still might preserve us in His name.

XVIII
Hope for Immortality Hinges on the Resurrection

It has always been obvious that this is the conundrum; such power as may work through us is ultimate, but the action we take is reserved, so as not to allow that power to dominate in the way the world understands. For He who reaps where He did not sow, enraged, would take what little was allotted back. All this, and what has been said, and what will be said, is for nothing if this creaturely existence be but our expected home, the final destination. We are pilgrims; and our hope is that our Friend, who entered into the realm of us who bear this Idea of love, could not be retained by that very creation which drove iron through His hands and feet. The rolled-away stone stands not as proof for you and for many, but for us is an icon formed by testimony and reason, without which our sense would evaporate. If we were to argue for the Absolute in terms of gradation or design, you would offer some counter-response; this, then, is why we seek no such proof to convince. Yet we do say, in respect of demonstrations from effect to cause, which the Subtle Doctor has attempted to define as a "threefold primacy," that we should allow the simpler contention to remain, that an impasse is reached: either something came from something, as we hold; or indeed something did come from nothing as you hold. You see that both presuppose a foundational fulcrum which vacates your empirical taste. In like manner, the resurrection of our Friend stands in primacy as doctrine, the axis of our hope; which, in this life, is not formed by the brackets of eros and thanatos. That is the Word of the Absolute, and by His Word, all things are possible.

XIX

Our Hope is Not a False Hope

It is acknowledged that the Compromised have offered incorruptibility to fallen followers as justification of blessedness; but such hope rests on the shoulders of those who require tangible saintliness as causes for intangible devotion. It is for that very reason that the Radicals have despised the other-worldly elements of the tradition, finding them intangible explanations for as yet unknown tangible causes. Those of the former, who desire to hold to the afterlife, seek signs; those of the latter, who leave what lies ahead to a rational calculation, seek action. Both, like bees, produce honey laced with the fragrance of flowers nearest their hives; and then, with feigned contemplation, pretend that the familiar scent is itself evidence of such a choice, and thus vindication. One has unwittingly framed the ideas as a mere tautology; the other has called such facts as offering nothing beyond a conjunction formed by habit.

What then for us, the Weak, who stand to account for this hope I just pleaded, the resurrection? that after the body dissolves into the ground, as a seed anticipating growth, there is offered again the return of such a growth which once more is nourished in the light, where for us the soul and body will in hope reunite? Each of us as creations retains all the elements of our form, not differentiated by the body, but with the body united and individualized; as in the case of our friend, the form, once returned, will again be recognized as a person who once lived, not as form void of matter. Did not Dante, upon seeing Peter, John, and James, know them by form complete, prior to wit and will, yet united in eternity?

Then, in line with, and not contrary to, the hope which was secured by our Friend, whom the vault could not keep, and who was first recognized by Magdalene as He, the same who was on the tree just three days prior, I ask: will not this same gratuity of physicality be extended to us by His friendship; cannot His lot be our lot? We could not believe in the prior without the former necessarily being true. Since no conviction of ours may be shaken by a mere dismissal, our Friend, who was carried into the tomb, walked by His own power freely into the morning air; breath and life returned. Then neither shall our hope, by you or the world, be called false if the claim of everlasting life seems improbable or impossible to those who cling to this world, of which such vision cannot glimpse farther than their last breath of their first life. Let the Compromised confront their control of the world; and, like the Radicals, may each confront their transparent desire for the very thing they publicly disdain, and may you, Secretary, clearly see the lack of hypocrisy in our Weakness.

XX

Earthly Possessions in Any Form Detract

You recall that Justin wrote of Sibyl and Hystaspes that the extermination of the corrupt will happen by fire; and that Plato held that one's form would never meet death, but traverses to spirit weighed down by adherence to this world, for which reason he held that such burial grounds remain where phantoms hover. Socrates, whom it displeased to see forms attached to the present world, fled not from his own impiety when he granted a cock to Asclepius, and unlike Homer, who laid two casks at the foot of Zeus, he found in gods, not many, but only one, the good. The Philosopher, likewise, offered two figures of the cosmos in human form, one temporal to this world, and yet the perfect which boasts no origin, equal to the Absolute in all but essence. Yet the vacuum, which nature abhors, unceasingly seeks satisfaction by proxy; as gaps are filled by desire for completion. Sextus the Pyrrhonist placed judgment aside, rendering a hollow worship; Spinoza found delight in the art, but not the artist; Nietzsche's lament of the death of certainty was but the rational outcry of dismissing the Absolute; and did not Minji Park affirm for compromise's sake that, on her account, the trivial should have its due, provided that no harm of order was brought to the social domain?

What I, and I pray you, find in these travesties is nothing save the inadequate mimicry of hope, articulated in temporal terms. The Compromised speak of societal love while stealthily embracing the market effect they publicly loathe, the source of the poor man's envy of the rich; the Radicals march towards societal change, while *sub rosa*, they squeeze each ounce of market utility from the society yet formed by their marching plans, the source of the poor man's uprising over the rich. This sinister reversal is offensive to reason and Reason; our own cynicism but preserves sanity from constantly trying to call attention to the obvious.

XXI

Substitute Systems Fail to Assimilate Truth

Allow further explanation as to why these parallel humanisms are complicit in each other's errors; and, by that, offer no respite given but solely what our Friend has disclosed in His incarnate presence as the God-Man. One such reason has just been provided: the fatiguing effect of arguing trivial matters that do not conflict with any central point, but are driven by ideologies undetected or ignored. Let not the following illustration exhaust your patience, but its logic, or lack thereof, is not apparent to many. Here is my example: I have used the term *man* equivocally, but in hopes that such clarity arrives by reference. In Genesis, context is the case; for the Hebrew term *adam*, as unspecified, connotes not *male*, but *mankind*; or to what purpose would man "created in His image," if it were used to mean male, immediately be followed by the phrase, "male and female He created them," if not that *adam* refers equally to both. And further it doubles as plural and singular: *adam* as mankind, or *adam* as this human. Yet for some in our contemporary period, man, as exclusive, excludes by extension the more sublime sex, the female; and therefore it is thought a discriminatory word.

Even within culture, as etymology attests, man is to be held of the human race entire: the rebuttal appears, as sometimes happens, in the very term used to make the illicit conclusion. This means that as the term human in general contains the portion, man—read more clearly as hu-man—when this is erroneously thought to pertain only to the male, no one argues that women, as wo-men, are not hu-man. Therefore "human" holds meaning for both sexes, male and female. The problem would not be solved by arguing that an odd substitute, such as "hu-women," might rectify the concern, as it itself would continue to suffer from the same illogic that the so-called problematic term, man, stubbornly retains in that hoped-for neologism. My point is to illustrate, you see, how contending with trivial matters becomes wearisome. The point here at present is that as one defense ensues with clear points and arguments sound, manufactured offenses drag the discussion into weeds and quicksand. They do this not for limpidity, but only, by hiding transparency, to obscure their weak logical stance.

Optimistically, then, if I have sufficiently addressed such an obstacle, with what I call the Idea of the human, this nature finds no birth in nature; our Friend likewise, though within and from the God-Bearer-Woman, was alone conceived extratemporally by the Love which transcends world and time. The substitutes of such natures then, with weeds removed and feet on firm soil, can be exposed. Allow me now to apply this drawn-out logic, free from any synthetic incense diverting constructive dialogue, in hopes that agreeable dispositions would not seek the fallacy, and would allow the essential arguments to bear all the focus.

Here is the case. The Compromised shun hoarding of property, but in sad irony lest it be placed by trustee in their hands, and they present themselves as distributors of justice, daring anyone to argue that they are not, at least, doing good. Then the Radicals shun the hoarding of property, lest, like the Compromised, their enlightened souls manage sole custody, and present themselves as managers of justice, daring anyone to argue that they are not, at least, creating good. In either case, the few govern the many, forgetting that King spoke of philanthropy as the response of the rich to social injustice; and thus in either expression, the elite elect themselves to speak for the commoner. Finally, in a twisted hope, the self-appointed stewards appear masquerading as lords, where the Compromised speak of only one lord and the Radicals shun all lords. Then each, in their cloaked aristocracy, rules. The commoners, who are but rabble, thought not capable of understanding the chosen vision of each, are asked to submit to better judgments: these flowers of society hold in disdain those very people they claim to enshrine but nonetheless deem unworthy of such poignant insights. The Compromised manage only to pick the soul's pockets of those driven under their shepherding, as to govern the holy needs of the elite; and the so-called Radicals, with contempt for those identified as insipid, interpret the commoners' convoluted lofty thoughts with such conflated language that vagueness becomes the plot to crown their own ideological needs.

Each humanist trend has distinct means, and each shares but one final end: the substitution of truth for expediency, and, from that, the propriety to control. This is a disruption of human nature, foreign to the mind of holiness that the Weak have endeavored to sustain, and devolving the spirit of Love's mercy and hope to the remnants left over from overfilled exhibitions and egos. To add further insult, we are supposed to accept each respectfully as good-doers and good-thinkers. They have equivocated terms, but the Weak will not equivocate truth so as merely to appear, as others outside the truth are so quick to say, to be on the right side of history.

XXII
Why Our Faith and Precarity Remain True

Recall what we uphold. The Weak submit that the Absolute by breath created all: our Friend, the Breath from Heaven, lovingly situated Himself in our low human state, enjoining a nature logically incapable of containing such a form to recreate all that otherwise could not obtain such Form. The spirit of Love, like the sun and rain which nourishes, carving hearts like landscapes, ever sustains and replenishes, thus falling on all. What is beyond these elements lovingly given should not be freely received; and by that, this is sufficient to sustain man, the pinnacle of the Absolute's gifts, and whose each nature is welded by Him to eternity. You asked what distinguishes us from the Compromised and Radicals, and again I say precarity. Our instability allows us to rest in the power of others' ability, and we know that they have received such by the utterance of the Absolute. See, all those goods that are given were never theirs, but to all through them, to whom His love works on our behalf, this idea of Being is an ontological solidarity, that in justice extends to the body whole. We accept materials secondhand, and it is said that what is secondhand can only be so because another had it first, as firsthand, acquired as new and unspoiled belongings that their worldly pursuits permitted them to purchase, and thus our gain, which trickles from their own. If that remains your critique, Secretary, that our sustenance is only capable of expression by another's fortune, without whom we could not maintain our precarity, then you have yet to understand the Weak; and, secondly, you are not the first to levy it against us.

In fact, the Weak is a name given to us disparagingly. We assembled earlier as the Poor, of whom our brother Luke spoke as the Blessed to inherit the kingdom of God; but since we seek what we do not have from those that do, the other sects found our argument a weak way to assure piety. Now we assent to that degradation, and cheerfully find it both risible and applicable; the jest has become our banner. But now let me state further that, more importantly, you do not understand the affluent from whose firsthand goods we pick, which you are counted among, that you, and all, are unwittingly still both deeply loved and used for His will in us; though it is not for us, but for you, and Him. We are all utterly incomplete, and these material findings serve only utility and pleasure; satisfying merely the corporeal aspects of our being. For you, myself, and all, let us make a single plea: finish what you have begun in us, oh Lord, as you draw all things to Thee; may that be our sign to you and the world's kingdom.

XXIII

The Remnant Calls Him Friend

We are Weak; weak for the many, because our Friend was weak for all; in holy irony He was weak for all, yet not many seek His weakness. Yet we take heart, as should you, Secretary, that though His garments were divided, His tunic remained seamless. So, too, even if we are divided, His love for all remains seamless. The Weak stand as a remnant of this truth, until by irresistible Love, all are made whole in eternal life, where, upon encountering the Absolute, each heart will toil like Penelope's Web being made ready to receive Love in fullness. This paradox is not lost, in that we, the Weak, display a truth which both the Compromised and Radicals claim as whole, but each has absconded by attachments to power. Whether power is used to adorn authority, or to distribute as forced justice, no difference remains: each, like wispy smoke, attempts to assume a form of which neither is capable. Furthermore, as lip service—though they deny this—both claim to evidence what only the Weak can authentically signify to the kingdom. The Weak, neither claiming a truth exclusive, nor broadening a truth inclusive, can portray faith and reason as a single truth by life's witness, which, in itself, becomes an icon of the Immortal.

The Absolute, again, is not taken by sheer appearance. Did not Samuel have seven sons from which to choose, the number of perfection, yet to David, not among them, was given the blessing? And did not our Friend send His disciples out two by two, the number of the faithful, with only staff in hand, not to subvert the political arena, but, with neither money nor bread, to command authority over spirits unclean? So too, our Friend, the One Son, issued forth from the Three, the number of wholeness, as perfection from perfection; and by such, hearts are subverted, and spirits made clean if only they assume the weakness He in nativity bore.

XXIV

Contrived Signs & Boasting Affiliations

You see then the line of truth which has been found within revelation, both divulged as predictive prophesy and testified to as exhibited evidence. With this line, the Weak stand as a stalwart symbol of the good. The Compromised hate us for this, for we bear openly their cloaked affliction, and the world hates words void of witness; the Radicals despise us for this as we bear joyfully their pronounced evil, and the world despises words mismatch to witness. Both use idols as phrases, and phrases formed as idols. Each delivers admiration only to seek its return from the lips of origin—a narcissistic tendency to praise close friends for the sole elevation of the self. One has the token of moral superiority, which neither scandal nor elevation has deadened by desire; the other has elevated empirical science under the guise of revealed wisdom, and their ubiquitous academic presence cannot quench their thirst for seats of privileged opinions. Esteemed by some, these spiritually-weak seek signs, and the proud boast of their affiliations. They have become Lewis's men without chests: inordinately large heads thought of such high acumen, with stomachs bloated by publications and pomp. Their shrunken chests lack the mediating virtues of honor and courage, making the chest and abdomen only appear more developed; in truth both are chestless. This, good Secretary, is the foretelling which has now come to pass; let this be my response to the question your Ministers have put to the Weak, as to why we claim to be an icon of the good.

XXV

Good is Tethered to Reality

What, then, underlies the rise of this phenomenon? It is social experience that placates the Compromised and vindicates the Radicals. Forced into debates of years past, the Radicals intersected social kinds to vacate those things called natural; the Compromised were numbed both in soul and mouth as if prodded by a torpedo-fish; paralyzed, they repeat tired phrases. It is said that division widens when the soul is angry: when enraged, one seeks confirmation of their point, regardless of veracity. Yet the anxious soul strives to seek the truth; and in it, resolution narrows the partisanship of ideas. Here, the Radicals endeavor to confirm their bias, while the Compromised repeat conventional lines that echo their catechesis.

So, the Compromised resist any taxonomic flattening, but offer little other than tasty words that their like will attempt to swallow, but which in truth congeal, like cold fat in the throat of culture. The Radicals awarded the essential to the social, where experience in the world confirmed that such was real: the effect remains real, even if the idea remains mind-dependent. Here, once more, there have arisen errors of excess and deficiency; and Scotus reorients this primal good in terms of arguments necessary and natural (one is demonstrable, the other prior to such demonstration). The nature of a thing is derived from what is necessary. Be there volition or mind: each presents first as self-evident to all beings with rationality and will, and these twin powers terminate in love. The formal distinction remains: even as powers are permitted distinct status, the first Tablet provides what is endowed to the human person, and presents it as real; for the human person is necessarily tethered to such an authentic good. The Weak accept this.

XXVI

Value and Utility are Modern Magic

With the good untethered from the necessary, what is prescribed as desired interest becomes determined as care; the perceived good takes on the properties of value and utility. Those considered future people; who lack consciousness; were euthanized dependent on factors of genetic fitness. The days of Sanger had returned, but in a more serious and subtle form. The failed melting pot was sieved once more: technology allowed an insight that the surface phenotypes of past observation did not permit. Though even artificial intelligence did not allow the conjuring of a perfect purpose, factors unearthed in testing set the path for societal values to maintain the goal of a prejudice that, like an inflated ball held underwater, simply finds the surface elsewhere, in an area distant, or not, from where it was first pressed down. Then too with the elderly, infirm, and disabled; when such utility leaves their horizon the surfacing ball became visible, and even involuntary means were brought to bear on those cases. For when will and care were found in scant amount, instead of juggling resources or impinging on one's lifestyle, society moved to sustain the values of the influential and able. Yet now, who but the Weak champion the causes of the marginalized who did not fit the parameters of the Radical's fashionable offences; or the value of even genetic diversity that the Compromised failed to address with moral scandal as the lens, thus leaving licit positions logically untenable? The Weak reject such as modern magic, and pray, in spirit and deed, to temper its societal spell.

XXVII

Dignity is Pinned to Personhood

Your Ministers have informed you that we admit the young and old as they are, impaired and infirm, in the name of our Friend, who insists that all are accepted, not because of those infirmities or impairments, but without regard to such. Yet the error we hear from you is that the infirmity or the impairment is the will of our Friend. This is lunacy. It was first among us, the Weak, that modern care arose; yet we attempted a restoration of wit and function, not a replacement of treatment with a sacrifice and extinction predicated on value and utility. The Weak sacrifice themselves, and seek only the extinction of that which diminishes the person; we will not sacrifice others for our own well-being. We have persistently made the case that both life and humanity are quantifiable; the Compromised and Radicals hold to that also; but for us, personhood is qualitative and necessarily pinned to all human life.

The Compromised, by our witness, hold this, but argue wrongly that at both ends of the spectrum, it is life itself which is sacred. Though there is truth embedded in that notion, it is indefensible, as there is no controversy in it, for the world understands the biological supposition that life precedes personhood. The Radicals too agree with our premises; but fail to extend the quality of personhood to that which is quantifiable, and thus personhood becomes a functional appraisal. There is but one valid and sound conclusion that follows from our argument: either every living human is a person, or only some living humans are persons, and to that one adds value. If there is a third position, say what it is. If that is not the sole point to address, say what it is. Here, the culprit is only indirectly attributed to power, for that ultimate good is regulated by such currency as the kingdom of this world seeks: utility and value; and the power which the State holds as its own. Where expense is curtailed to preserve utility, power expands. To the extent which personhood is controlled by desirable values, resources are retained.

XXVIII

False Freedom is a Digestible Lie

We do not identify with our persecution, nor make light of it; yet there is an analogy between the Weak and the historically pious figure named Job, who, a foreigner to the Absolute, like some Greeks, followed the Way of the Absolute. We by fortune of time differ from Job, however, in that we do know the Way, and follow it intentionally. We, the Weak, solicit Job's heroic patience, who in his time endured such physical and emotional pangs, inflicted by the Adversary, with the Absolute's shield dispossessed, as both virtue tempered and witness accentuated. This Job, whom Sirach speaks of as "he who held fast to justice," wavered not, and this man of justice did not seek recompense or count unjust what was allowed to transpire in his life. He did not seek immediate remedy in accord with utility, or count such misery as mere inconvenient value. This stands as testimony against unbridled freedom, which, good Secretary, you and the kingdom hold to be lack of restraint or the absence of imposition. In the time of Job, as now, it is the Great Liar who dictates this pretense, and declares the subtlety of autonomy to be the rational dictate of human will. If by nature a human life is granted personhood, then it must follow that any freedom espoused by utility and value is in direct opposition to that design; this is gleaned by reason, by which alone excellence is found and celebrated as virtue.

XXIX

Freedom is Bounded by Necessity

But cunning is this Great Liar, not in directly tempting those whom the Absolute dearly loves, but in disengaging the human faculties so that the obvious is presented as imperceptible, and the explicit end made obscure; so that if even one false premise as a link is dislodged, the course becomes irreversible, and the questionable by default becomes conclusive; and, lastly, now as enshrined truth, is proffered as if it were authenticity and generosity. Whether it be in terms of the relational covenant, care for the unconscious, or the unwanted, or, in the converse case, with designed genetic expressions, to thwart what is required is not rebuttal, but to promote the unoriented, and the undetermined initial premises, as oblique but palatable. With boundaries not explicitly erased, but reformed and packaged to fit the pliable desires and values of societal exchange, what remained to take the place of the discarded nature but the struggle of Sisyphus, which provided a mirage of relief from an existence otherwise intolerable? When a definition is confirmed, does not the confinement of such a term seek freedom within those bounds? For outside both heat and light, by what necessity does a candle burn, as no candle is free to burn or offer heat when submerged in water? No, for such autonomy has then but sought ends not bounded by necessity.

And, to reiterate, that is why the Weak are hated. We alone have clearly announced the absurdity of such a hopeless task when applied to what is clearly present in the design of a person; it was said by Desmond, "Woe be the day when such a being as Sisyphus comes to realize their condition"; but let me add, "Woe to them who are found to disclose such pitiable enlightenment," requiring Sisyphus to confront such redundant absurdity. The grass was not found greener on the other side of their cultural fence, but because it was thought so, the newly experienced grass remained desired. Yet once the fence was crossed, to leave the illusion unfulfilled became more tolerable than admitting the falsehood. Once the falsehood is accepted, it is easier to affirm than to deny it; and the greater the company one keeps in such a shared mirage, the more easily the lie, now communal, convinces the masses whose emotions have been manufactured to conform. In Stockholm fashion, all have bonded with their captor experiences, fulfilled by expectations. This is how deviance triumphs where, otherwise, disdain for error would open up the recognition that only by an illicit formation does such a discovered nature allow manipulation to become mutable or expendable.

XXX

Desire Limits Veracity

This prevalence of conformity is the step-child of misplaced desire. Shaped by accommodation or progressive design, it emerges as that societal spell; then, whether the temptation is one of omission or of commission, I intend to lay these claims bare in my prose, and justify my own approach. I do concede, that unlike our Friend, who did not force conviction of His love on all, out of respect for our limited nature, I cannot force conviction of His love even upon any, because of my own limitations. As I proceed to connect events following a historical timeline, as staccato-like threaded details—in fact, multifactorial—it can wrongly suggest that successive events must necessarily be causally connected. But having offered that proviso, I will presumptively indulge your assimilation to the evidence given as apology alone, and carry on, at the risk of over-simplifying my chronicling. As Chesterton put it: "if a thing is worth doing, it is worth doing badly." And though different by kind, if our Incarnate Friend did not seek to satisfy the desires of all peoples, allow me, who am nothing, General Secretary, to seek merely the satisfaction your desire examines of our plight.

XXXI

Our Heritage is Revolt and Resistance

As recorded in the history of our heritage, the Absolute has raised up foretellers who stand as witness to His single, unfolding truth; to the Father of Faith, Abraham, a Servant, our Friend, would be raised up; then an improbably capable man, Moses, was sent to Egypt, heralding the release of God's captive peoples. In the desert, they were formed into a nation testifying to His love, and, like our Friend, the serpent was raised to save the inflicted; resisting the lure of worldly kingdoms, the Absolute was hesitant to raise among them one who would reign; but a prophet king was anointed, from whose flesh and blood it was foretold that an eternal king would be brought forth. After the days of Wisdom, generations of silence fell upon the chosen; and as sun beams pierce the crevice of a dwelling when morning breaks, Isaiah foretold the virgin Woman, who, without hesitancy, presented her womb, welcoming the new covenant; at this annunciation the Word was made flesh. The Word, from nativity to maturity, grew in stature and wisdom. Then, in self-revelation according to John, our Friend announced His mission at the well to an unlikely woman; Mark had the challenge of giving the one thing lacked, all of his possessions to the poor, and, with gentle spirit, "looking upon him, loved him" in spite of the sorrow felt.

Our Friend enjoined all to love and understand with their hearts, but so as to vindicate such promise; on the Sabbath He healed the withered hand, and one was brought back to wholeness with merely the touch of His garment, from which a spirit issued forth. The blind came to see, while those nearby with sight became blind, and the mute were given speech while others with tongue were made silent. The enmity placed between the woman and the serpent became the enmity between the Way and the world; nothing remained hidden; all was made bare. Our revolt and resistance mirrors that of the great prophets; may generations a thousand years from now find solace in our faithfulness; may our story be added to this chorus.

XXXII

Our Friend Predicted the Status of the Weak

Why then, you ask, are not these points, though plain to a mature mind, no justification for even theoretical exoneration? The response is predicated on the thorny mantle we prescribe as the antidote to an assimilation to power and pretense. Our Friend was Truth, and did not simply speak truth, as I am attempting here. Yet this Truth wore a wreath of spines and brambles, while the world of His time sought a liberator donning a crown of precious metals and jewels; people find more readily what satisfies their search, rather than that which satisfies the truth. The Compromised mark their elite with tiaras and miter; the Radicals divulge their poorly concealed aristocracy by a garland of degrees and coronet recognitions.

We, for our part, will have none of it. The Rich Ruler did not become genuinely rich until dispossessed of the many priorities which tied him down; like the shackles on Dickens's fetter-drawn Marley, they will not, in this life, come to recompense. By what logic could we claim otherwise, but by not following our Friend, and accepting His crown; of whom Paul warned that, though He was rich, yet He for our sake became poor, so that we through His poverty might become rich in everlasting liberation. The very same Word that inspired the Prophets of the Absolute, and the disciples of our Friend, is present with us now, and with me presently, as the spirit of Love which communicates truth disinterestedly; it rains on all, even if some refuse to admit it.

The spirit of Love replenishes our strength to overtake our weaknesses; so, to apply our Friend's consolation, we, the Weak were not the first hated. And may I humbly add that this hatred, stemming from our distance from the world, is the only measurable wreath which appropriately resembles our King's crown in this life. It is our willing mantle.

XXXIII

The Weak Are Content to Wear Down Errors

It remains an aporia to me, and all the Weak, why anything other than what was just offered could be thought unpredictable. The foretelling that anticipated the birth our Friend, and His reception during public life, was set; those who adhere to the Way for the sake of the Absolute, are present to the worldly kingdom in and by Him; then our own inception and societal rejection follows, given that it is His faith we express; should not the Weak in the world now likewise anticipate the same portion as our Friend? The prediction of His ordeal, followed by ample fulfilment, stands as testimony to the authenticity of the Weak; it is the concealment, coupled by false pretense—which should concern your honorable status—that falls to the lot of the Compromised and the Radicals. By adapting to the culture, content with the shadows they call reality, as that by some measure which finds favor with the State, they stand to lose all if their contrived stance is exposed. We, who are Weak, hide nothing; and by hiding nothing, leave nothing to unmask. Isaiah foretold that our Incarnate Friend would neither shout, nor cry out, nor raise His voice in the streets; neither do we, the Weak, shout, or cry out, or raise our voices in the streets.

But then we, like our Friend, have allowed this response to expected instigation, or in fact, our inaction with respect to such, to become the very paradoxical thing which draws attention to ourselves; and thus, it has left our backs open to stripes, again, not unlike our Friend and Lord—but only to the degree that our nature and constitution tolerates. The prophecy of the Lamb followed the instantiation of His sacrifice; now, as His prophecy is ours, so too now His plighted reward is ours. The Angel of God came to the God-Bearer; overshadowing her, the Word arrived as a quiet Being, a calm, spoken Word. Angelic hosts on heaven's edge, in anxious hope, begged a "yes" from the Maid; and by such fiat our Lord processed forth. What danger was in that? The powers feared the turning of the world; in prophecy, what was thought to follow, but a revolt, culminating in an established throne, and a like kingdom; by this, they schemed, claiming those Holy Innocents. Spared by Heaven's Love, our Lord matured, for thirty years in private, and three more in public. Even then, the Word remained quiet to revolt; as, of the counterparts of that time, the Compromised desired leisure and thus favored stability, and the Radicals desired revolution and thus favored zeal. Both feared the growing movement of Love, a benevolent foe.

Our Friend, and His transformative words, were like water dripping slowly on the rock of established powers and prestige; unnoticeable except in the depression it was carving into hatred and indifference, a depression that would only deepen over time. Love grew proportionate to the depth of wear, and time was on the side of the timeless. So, presently, in the same way, what danger then can we, the Weak, be to you, save that more time has passed, and our adherence to this Love continues the erosion of the world's falsity and odious ideas? If evil is the privation of Love such as being in us, in you, then, the idea of Love is the negation of deception and hate. The Apostle Mark wrote that our Friend commanded His disciples to take nothing for their journey except a staff and cloak; no bread, no bag, no money in their belts. Has not our precarity borne this out? Has not such an ordinance continued in our lives?

Responding to our Friend's call to the Rich Ruler by our very lives, has not our voluntary choice to give all that we have, that which brought him sadness, for us brought joy? Judge if our lives now have become the visible love of our Friend, who is invisible otherwise to you and I both. In our adherence to the Way, Love is made visible to the world; the world scorns such precarity, as they had scorned our Friend's lowly state; the threat appears in the unexpected response, and, seeking Love rather than power and prestige, thwarts the world's imagination, and, with suspicion converted to conviction, the world hates what it cannot comprehend. In us, Love remains in the world as a Child, who seeks no power or prestige, in the same manner that a tender Child, birthed in a cave of Bethlehem, was but the Absolute's whisper of the spirit of Love, proffering nothing except a revolution of tenderness. I hold that the way of the Weak, as children of Love in the world, but not of the world, was clearly foretold, and is, for you, presently, fulfilled in plain sight.

XXXIV
The Origins of Persecution are Well Known to Us

The Weak are not clever, and I, the least among them; but we do boast a shield preserving us within Love's enduring hold, which, according to the Liar's jest, offers no promise of comfort and protection. We embrace poverty; but, as stated, are mocked for having the means to achieve material compensation and what is thought to flow from that, consolation in this world. Yet in choosing not to do so, we uncover a dichotomy which the Compromised and Radicals exploit. In terms of our mission, it is thought patronizing to assume the lowly status voluntarily while so many enter into poverty without choice, lacking any avenue of escape that we willingly travel on. But did not Day herself stumble on this conundrum? Her precarity was chosen, and the woman was put to the curb with all her earthly belongings, which were but a few—put there because of circumstances that, if possible, she, and all sensible souls would avoid. Further, no provisions are made by us for future care and concern, and then, in want, our elderly days are spent.

But listen! Did not the holy Physician tell of such a warning—that those who have ample goods laid up for many years, will not be aided by them in the afterlife, becoming the property of others when the unexpected day arrives? What was preparation for life was ill-preparation for eternal life. Consider the Prayer our Friend taught us—"give us today our daily bread"—but the Compromised store enough bread for years of expected life, for travel and leisure; and the Radicals make full use of the bread from goods that they cavalierly denounce, ironically also for travel and leisure. The former feeds on usury with proceeds from vast swaths of property, and the latter feeds off the successful who denounce such with impunity, each thinking the propagandized distance between them and the source of wealth exonerating. We, on our part, know the blessings of the goods we receive openly, accept them graciously, and pass them on to others, when our dignity is complete. Again, notice the pattern: we do willingly what the Compromised exhort others to do, but do not do willingly themselves; and we do willingly what the Radicals expect others to do, but do not do willingly themselves. The Weak have no clever skills in such scheming games of investment and acquisition, nor do the Weak wish to contribute to the feigned disdain of such champagne collectivists. Let this then, our unearthly wisdom, witness that, in the company of the clever and worldly, we neither have for ourselves nor seek any advantage, be it material or cultural; we are content both in and with Love, and not for tomorrow's bread.

XXXV

The Weak's Plea is a Testimony of Contrast

Since the time of Malthus, control of the masses was deemed a prudent tool of the crafty to reach morally compulsive ends; instinctually, then, as always, the sorting favored those deemed suitable to societal values and the course of actions, which then, as always, were determined by those with power. Followers of Northern Europe set aside *prima scriptura* as a principle to align with the Thoroughbreds; the Weak knew that the melting pot would be the target of such a sinister cabal. Assembly line production called both men and women from their home shops; men were placed in the factories to do by specialization in a day what otherwise required weeks of one man's labor; with child removed from the breast, women were pulled from the household economy, to disciplined and divided labor, producing clothing at a fraction of the cost-burden anyone could do by their own effort. The capitalist-conformist man used fashion and possessions to herald such progress; as the bourgeois women, confined to their luxury, amused themselves with their convenience. Such advantage for the few placed a mantle on the destitute producers; who were, in truth, producing destruction to their nature. The unproductive lozenge issued first to those who were unfit, and thus, by such twice-cursed, determined to make them infertile, and so prevent such lowly creatures from breeding. Not only were they sent to join their husbands outside the home under the guise of liberation, but under the guise of liberation, too, they were aided by science to reduce the ranks of their unfitness.

The Radicals embraced this voluntary motherlessness, and, with scientific skill found that the origin of such a species need not be susceptible to misguided parentage. The Compromised pushed back with earnest effort, to the Radicals' chagrin; but their efforts ignorantly merged as, in various ways, the Compromised alienated the woman with a theology for their own gain, as silencing can achieve the same result as lessening. Multifariously, the Compromised placated their ideology with conformity; multifariously, the Radicals placated their ideology with liberty, each for their own advantage. While this unproductive medicinal lozenge allowed the female to imitate the male, by sinister serendipity, emotion increased attraction, and confused the latter with love, and affective pairing. As the female was now chemically sterile, this affected, too, the incalculable olfactory role; the selection of the other not just by sight but scent was removed, masking those elements of fertility compatible with immunity. In an irenic irony, the female was biologically forced to choose partners who were unfit for her. Each denatured woman was targeted with the subtle promise, as if by perverse reversal the God-Bearer could be convinced to respond "let it *not* be done according to thy will"; many, with that shallow promise, were drawn from the home and thus, the family was quartered. Medicine to induce infertility indeed made them infertile not only by a reduction of libido, but perpetual infertility ensued as an effect. And two further sad results are engendered by this so-called progress: that the female, once established with mate and family, with discontinued use of this unproductive medicinal lozenge, found that their choice in partner no longer matched their desire; then, secondly, with genes suppressed, reduced satisfaction bears the brunt of what became the rise of infidelity.

Would the Radicals have recognized their quasi-activism, like social posts of the past, serving only to decorate their feeds as a performative act? Their cry for social change, to raise the family out of poverty, induced only the self-importance of their selves, liberated from nature. The Compromised, never accepting the Weak's plea for their leaders to occupy such a low residence as in the poorest of their parishes, began to model in kind the antithesis of the Weak's domestic church, as their moral authority was torn asunder by their concealed plots of power and sex deviance unveiled. We were heralds to this demise; the Weak stood as the standard against such assimilation; our quiet resistance was drowned out by a power and ideology too stern to shift. Rumblings and failings, eugenics spread from nation to nation, to a united clerical silence adopted in hopes of avoiding loss of influence, which loss, to their minds, would be the only genuine scandal; whereas we, who are not of this world, remained a beacon to courage and honor. The signs were clear for all with eyes to see; but as the Father from Hippo has said, one needs not just eyes to see, but eyes which are fit to see. The cultural conspirators both yielded to sociosexual urges, and, to validate their shortcomings, ratified this frailty by adopting such impotence; it is, in short, an ethic of concession elevated to an imperative. "All that glitters is not gold" means that some things that glitter are gold, but also in logical form that some things that glitter are not gold. Precarity does not seek that which glitters, and thus is preserved from the false promise of gold.

XXXVI

Love Works Towards the Needed Good

Yet this muted plea, shared as word and sign, is, by nature, found in both those in the world, and those of the world; beloved John said that for those born of the spirit of Love, it blows as a wind where it wills. Many hear its sound, but many know not whence it came or whither it goes. And we know that the spirit of Love enters those whom Love chooses, to the extent that they cooperate with His idea of Love, for it is a nature reserved from none. And at all times the Absolute has chosen not merely from those who love Him, but from others who love Him but know Him explicitly not; where even then in His Love they are chosen as His.

But some examples from the course of time include the following: Sophocles speaking through Antigone on burying her brother justified by what cannot, not be known; and Socrates recognizing the One, which by that embraces the irony of his State's atheism, and campaigns his own bodily demise. Or how Paul spoke of those having not the law, but becoming a law unto themselves; where Perpetua did not spare her father's grey hairs, and Justin held to the partakers of the Logos that stood outside their ranks. And even Saladin, the knight without fear or blame, did he not occupy the bank of Acheron? Nor, over the voice of the multitude, could Henry Tudor erase Beckett's shrine of gold; and there it has stood for nearly nine hundred years. And in turning back to rescue his pursuer through the ice, Willems embraced his fate without fear or pause, while both Stowe and Douglas, with single vision from contrary arms, defined the contours to abolish bondage of irons. And vindicated by time, the phenomenologist Stein did not hesitate, she whose brilliance, shown as ashes, rose from pyres of hatred; and Day resisted the collective mind for war, to let bombs fall and go inside no more. King, too, while braced on the shoulders of Randolph, participated in law by reason and conscience, as he sat in a cell for breaking the non-law in a letter he wrote; and then Babyak brought unity to a nature sewn in turmoil, foiling a resurgence of Huxley's oxygen-deprived Deltas and Epsilons. And in the days intellect was bestowed to machines, Abubakar raised the dignity of those for whom self-projection fulfilled Levy's forecast, where in the year twenty-fifty, pseudo-love formed as the desire for non-human companion and affection.

These are but a few notables of the spirit of Love, Easter's light, streaming through any window or crevice, to reveal the Absolute, for whom the human person is but Love's arena. If our Friend, as entering Jerusalem's gate, affirmed the spirit of Love speaking through the palm-brandishing multitude, saying that even the very stones would cry out if they did not. Then from human lips, with dignity more precious than granite, would not the idea of Love even be less suppressed? Consider at that time how others schemed destruction, for it was only one week from gate to tomb; yet the resurrection further confirmed as an eternal nature this idea of Love, that all now know that even time itself cannot suppress Love's return to the Absolute.

XXXVII

The Absolute Makes Truth Known

From crib to grave, in each generation Babel towers the world erected, and ever-ready responders were summoned. The arrogance, that this earth, which is but a foot stool to the Absolute, a fleeting moment to our Friend, and but a breath exhaled to the spirit of Love, was ventured by such contingent being the inverse of Creator and created!

Yet we, the created, climbed our double helix to be gods, and entangled the perplexities of violence with an aspiration to achieve such ends. Yet did not man's boastful ebb recede only before the Absolute's flow of mercy, greater mercy given with the unceasing tide as justice? Was not Mary's untying of the knot only to be superseded by our Friend's infinite elevation of the creature's finite nature, of which, in eternity, the God-Bearer tasted first? The Word speaks unity.

XXXVIII

Our Friend is the Icon of Truth and Love

This Word, by earthly mission called, who, from the lips of the Virgin's mouth, was summoned from the throne; who with the span of outstretched arms could gather the Sun and other stars, and have in His ring the new moon as a jewel, became for all, as Love, a living Sabbath. Our Friend's labor of mercy became our day of rest, removing any necessity for the blood of bulls and lambs, the giving of bread and wine; He sought only our submission to His Love, placed in each as an Idea, as beacons signaling His presence to and from each, drawing that which is of Him, back to the point of His omega. What dwelling could be worthy of this gift, save the human heart first created, then elevated, by the Uncreated?

Becoming the sacrifice once for all, no sacrifice would afterwards suffice; save that of now receiving in Bread and Wine our Friend, who, with us in sacrament, while not present in person, until we in heavenly rite will become one with Him as persons. His Sacrifice, once completed, now moves through those who stand for Him, to all the world, those He has fallen and crawled for; with Him being raised up; know I speak of all, and of you, great Secretary, who are raised in dignity and covered in mercy. The crucifix has become our symbol of gift, for on it hung our salvation; it is, for us too, a perpetual hope, our resurrection and icon of Love.

XXXIX

The Procession of Love Strikes Tongue and Heart

From the time of the Old Covenant, to the time at which the Word was spoken in Jerusalem; twelve who were chosen, one who failed, became the sturdy yeast of those who followed. As Tertullian explained, each martyr's demise became the seed, and thus the end became the beginning; blood begat life in the Early Church. Yet if dying for one's cause would by that fact alone produce expansion of one's creed, then Ti and Do's extraterrestrial venture would only have been the beginning and not the end of their pitiable brief movement; or Russel's Kingdom Hall followers, once a century past Jerusalem's established statehood, this generation of time then run dry, would not have been the death knell but rather their springtime of faith. It is not enough for even such bravery, as Cicero had claimed, to "Die boldly and those in your midst, inspired, will take up the herald"—a sign to follow. But the peoples of the world have swelled our ranks. Proceed forth: Love strikes tongue and heart to proclaim how truth and love manifest by our proliferation.

XL

How Love in the World is Made Known

From the original Twelve to this present day, where has this Love not spread; on what shore has its foot not set; in what language is the Truth not spoken; what ear has not heard the message? It is within the reach of all. If, for Britain, the sun never set on its empire, the claim was limited by known worlds; yet, with no corner now unknown, what night shades the tabernacle of our Friend. Over two millennia ago, blessed Simeon prayed *nunc dimittis*, and those words laid bare the truth of quiet rumblings, soon to become a torrent. Brought forth to separate good from evil, the world awaited this God-Man whose wisdom would cause the fig tree to wither, yet it was not without love for those Temple's people. All those who in knowledge resist this Love, will be as wheat, separated in the wind; to those who spurn His weakness and lowliness, and perversely claim for themselves power and prestige, they will perish until the days when, made whole by Love, errors are then laid bare; our Friend's hand will pull them from drowning in the waters when, at last, their faithless struggle is apparent to all. Then, with drained agency, elevated above their nature, they will be unearthed as rampant rot; the meaning which they spurned, again always present, will raise in those three days, soul separated from the body, a kindled spirit worthy of union. But what is inevitable remains disposed: the leaders of the Compromised heed the counsel of their civil lawyers before His gospel; the leaders of the Radicals, inverting ideology and truth, heed the counsel of their civil scholars before His gospel.

Truth for both is like clay, no matter how beautifully crafted, as words, dashed against the ground of certitude, shatter in its brittleness. The casket of gold is chosen for its desire, and those who have sought the law prior to Law choose it as their hope, and do indeed have their want fulfilled; of the casket of silver, the standards repudiated by the progressives as ill-gotten gain, surrender to their temptations of outlier pride, which by such advantage yield all that they deserve; but the Weak, with neither false resemblance nor guile elevated to virtue, nor with pretense shrouding conservative initiatives in liberal garments, neither glittering gold nor shining silver offer temptation over such radiance of risking this life for the perfection in another. Our fear is respect; and that justice which we willingly give is also that which is deserved, taking the form of despised lead. Not from fear does it originate as being right and just, but from the recognition that our Friend first loved us, and that that which is freely given is equally freely returned. It is by this, that His love, to be in the world, was made known, so that when this world passes, that love alone remains; and may we be found in His company.

XLI

Love is Tethered to Sacrifice and Mercy

The Weak realize—and you should also—that temptations of silver and gold are ever present. Recall that Poor Francis tied the Gospel to actions; only when necessary were we to use words and offer explication. In like manner with temporal delights: we are admonished to choose the few over the many, with such joy to find an abundance of things in the fewest of things. Where, outside of His presence, that extends to all spaces in and out of time, is such grace resistible? The nations make idols of preservation, and seek the reduction of things to that which can be known; whereas we know, in that our Friend has handed it on as such, that sacrifice is preferred to gain; and in mystery we accept that without possible resolution in this existence, the depths of His love far exceed demonstration. The imitation of our Friend seeks no distinct ends separate from His earthly experience of sacrifice; and of that of sacrifice, He first desires mercy.

XLII

The Weak Anticipated What Was Made Known

Of what such earthly experience then can be said, if by revelation and wit, the evil errors foreseen are by the Weak spoken of as though they have already been; it cannot, and so what was anticipated has now come to pass? That does not make our prediction divine, save that by divine wisdom it is evident what effect can be ascribed to each cause. It is our Friend who has shed light on this, and on what will come to pass in time; for we, on our part, explain by the application of what He revealed to us, as events which unfold in history. If David spoke in word and psalm of things yet to be, then the Twelve made those known to their present time, but David was the source; and the Weak, resisting cultural and spiritual errors by the light of knowing man's inability to resist power and prestige, what was foreseen was in prudence obvious to follow.

For when, during reason's expansion to usurp revealed truth, those before us recognized that, like a social pendulum, time would offer a return to centered reason; is this still not our own, making come to pass, now known as true, what was predicted through Love? Our hope is not in the future unknown, but remains in the God-Man known, and from His single act, all hope springs forth. It is for Love, and for those with this idea of Love. Who does that exclude? For all that has come to pass, and all will come to pass, is anticipated until by Love, all error and human power is subdued; then, in final anticipation, Love itself will be made known.

XLIII

The Essence is Revealed in Resistance

Ends are not determined; a nature is not malleable. Those not of the Weak, outside our fold, differ not only by application, yet also—if not wholly—by what they propose. The Radicals hold to natures in flux, but act in discord to such agency they hold as determined; the Compromised recognize free agency but act in discord to natural kinds they hold as determined. The Compromised hold to a nature in their ethic, but live not by it. The Radicals hold to a nature in their materialism, but do not export it to their ethic. I wish to convey to you, Secretary, how our contention is proved true by rebuff and trial; that is, our resistance demonstrates the truth by the remains which time reveals. First, if the human person had no ability to avoid error, then culpability would similarly be removed, in that only the disordered nature could be deemed responsible.

All appear to accept this physiologically: cancer or pathologies of the heart demonstrated as congenital solicit pity, free from guilt, whereas lifestyles clearly chosen because of weakness of will, attach the effect to culpability. Yet within determinism, guilt, honor, sorrow, and prestige are but shallow presentations of perhaps unknown causes. Frankfurt attempted to demonstrate compatibility; though, in his confusion, he conflated the internal and external causes as distinct; in truth, it matters not the origin of compulsion if the end is preordained by encounters and indecipherable laws of physics. The bookend groups of our fold substituted nature or distorted its effect; the feigned conscience of corporations donned the appeasement of benevolent goals adapted to societal preferences and called it their brand; and, likewise, the patronizing fundraisers opened their gala doors for donors eager to be seen, who sought pleasure when listed as benefactors in support of community causes. Both were eager to promote their charitable efforts with photographs and other means of promotion.

This, of course, was marketed in public relations fashion, testing the response and adapting the shape until, most pleasing to self and world, the good deed can be absorbed by each as an idol's gaze. Cats hunt the mouse by instinct, and recline on a chair according to opportunity, yet neither the mouse nor chair claim credit for what the cat does as determined. Trees grow according to their environment, yet neither the soil nor unshielded sun claim credit for what trees do as determined. For cat or tree, if either can be properly said to "do" what is mere instinct, what blame is ascribed if sustenance and leisure are lacking? We, though, with created ideas of Love, never submitting to the cultural pendulum, are saved by our adherence to that which a thing is by nature; which is us, and our creed remains fixed essentially. And the Weak—like all humans, but unlike cats or trees—by essence remain the resistance to manipulation of will. As soft stone is washed away by torrent and time, with denser stone exposed, what protrudes, as accidents removed, is then essentially revealed, and so too is man's nature, resistant to both torrent and time.

XLIV

Partial Truths of Politics and Heretics

I will now speak in defense of two facets of our Friend's faith, facets which we the Weak hold in full, that are shared only in part by either the Compromised and the Radicals. By virtue of their efforts, each holds to a truth which, although partially expressed, nonetheless points to the fullness in both what is retained by scrutiny, and what is not retained by error; though there is no half to be held, since each part lacks the whole, and when part is removed, as an accidental, no-thing is revealed. Consider now what I speak of, the twin virtues precarity facilitates, honor and courage, by which, to some degree and in some facet, love is unreservedly expressed. Those two virtues remain, held to what is both worth dying for and defending, each not as an end, but as a legitimate means; though nothing found worthy of the one, can be abandoned by the other.

The first is honor, that is expressed in justice, that which is due to another; and the second courage, expressed by pressing the ideal, that which is due to the Absolute. Justice is to be afforded those, who like us, share this idea of Being; and the ideal is preserved in circumstances to honor the perfection of the Absolute, which we in courage image. In regard to the partial parts, the Radicals seek justice, but by being proponents of social programs; yet, by doing so, experience shows that courage thus wanes, for they do not rise to the virtue in their own lives. The Compromised seek honor, but complete this task as proponents of ceremony; and likewise by doing so, in experience, honor is thus squandered as a virtue in their own lives. Where these two sects meet the Weak with these virtues is in the service of love to those with whom we all share creation, and that is to be lauded; where each depart, respectively, is that the political and social expressions inevitably, as Solzhenitsyn pointed out, are foundational errors born from, respectively, rationalistic humanism or humanistic autonomy. As to the former, the Compromised are political heretics, where moral scandal is equated with loss of money; to the latter, the Radicals are heretical politicos, where scandal is equated with gain of money.

The Weak, christened by such in the cultural fire, can, in precarity with money rightly used, more easily discern that to lose much is authentic gain; by it, in fact, we are made less important so that He can be made more important. This is the prophecy spoken to us; so with these words I prophesy to you. We ask that neither you, nor others, bend their ears and hearts to the earthly stigmata of adorned seduction, or to the titillation of cajoled baseness. We, the Weak, are content in persuading those whom our Friend brings to us, and count you, Secretary, among those few whom we desire. That you will find wisdom and reason in these words is something I will unequivocally defend; that you might find such wisdom and reason in these words would be something also for which I willingly would die.

XLV

Liturgy as Foretaste of the Eternal

Liturgy, then, is the essential summit. On the third day, unsealed from death's sting, our Friend conquered, by rising, the complicit God-killers—among whom, you should know, the Weak number themselves—and whom, with but one affirming thought from Him while in front of Pilate, those infinitely numbered angelic beings, poised at the edge of eternity awaiting notice, could have annihilated. Yet this God-man, in victory over death, in final tribute, yielded to His human nature, accepting death, and returning to the Absolute as the Lamb who was slain; and there He remains in the Triune presence, ever offering His single sacrificial event to the Absolute, bearing all the marks of His earthly pilgrimage.

The Absolute repeatedly receives this willing gift from this ever-present sacrificed God-Man, and the spirit of Love gathers and communicates this sacrifice to the Absolute. He receives it, and, in like manner, the spirit of Love gathers from the Absolute His unreserved Love, that is, all that He has, and returns it to our heavenly Friend; He receives it. This perpetual presentation of inter-giving and inter-receiving as the mutual donation of Love, from one God-Person to the other, in ceaseless sacrifice, is Liturgy; for the relation of the spirit of Love, the Absolute, and our Friend are but a mystery, as One God, in a perpetual, self-comprised orbiting consummation of Love. It is in this way that Liturgy is the created idea of Being entering into Love's eternal embrace; and the Liturgy, which was given to us in Love, is that which we enter into as our Love service while in the temporal kingdom of life. During the liturgy, in and with this consummation of Love, the temporal limitation is pierced by the eternal Love that, not bound by time, enters time; and we who are bound by time penetrate eternity by the power of Him who first Loved us.

It should be perplexing to you, and all, why there would be any hesitancy—or, even worse, obstinacy—on the part of those who express a desire to spend eternity with the Absolute, but find it inconvenient or burdensome to celebrate while in the here-and-now, that foretaste in our liturgy of Love. The Weak would risk death for such an earthly anticipation of what will be afforded eternally, after our souls enter the orbiting Love of His presence. The possession of eternal life is to be possessed in an eternal liturgy; the participation in this earthly liturgy is both preparation and preservation of Love's eternal embrace. Liturgy, as that space-time breach, is to touch the eternal now in our temporality.

XLVI

Love Prior to Creation

This eternal now, our future remembering—itself a notion limited by language—places the origin of this idea of Love, not before time, but outside of time; and thus, for both the Uncreated, and as Eternal Love, it can be stated that existence precedes time. The existent unchanging Love entered changing time. It holds, then, that when the first two humans were granted, not just their being, but consciousness of soul, it followed from Love, as the idea of being as Love did not itself proceed from consciousness; and, by this love as present in them, like an eternal torch once touched to those earthly creations, Love set fire to creation. Think on how this eternal truth embedded in man finds expression as an eternal idea.

In the Noahidic mythos, it was the ark of love preserving creation's good; with Abraham, such sacrificial love's preservation was afforded for all future generations; with Moses, a people was established and formed as a nation of love; but it was with the Davidic covenant, now come to pass, that our Friend and Lord, as heralded to the world, eternal Love, took form. And the Uncreated, entering the created, became the spark of Love, as Love now in the world, manifested as a Person; and thus the God who had become human, had attained, for the human creation, the potency of becoming a god. What remained, for our part, in de Chardin's agile account, was that by harnessing those energies of love, man will for a second time in this created world have discovered fire. This is how Love existed prior to creation; and how Love will now, until consummation, persist in creation.

XLVII

Gehenna Cannot Resist Love

The Weak hold that, at some point outside of time, no being will remain capable of resisting Love. It is clear to us that there is indeed a Gehenna; our Friend, while on pilgrimage spoke of it; but it is, equally, not clear that it remains occupied; of that our Friend while on pilgrimage, did not speak. Those of the Radicals dismiss the notion of universal eternal love; they retain only that which is palatable to their peers, who have elevated reason as the sole god, unilaterally inaugurating a pleasant truth of no necessary judgment over that which was revealed by the spirit of Love. Those of the Compromised dismiss the notion of universal eternal love in principle; they retain only that which is palatable to retributions that have become attached to their prohibited violations, unilaterally inaugurating their unauthorized truth of judgment as separation, over that which was revealed by the spirit of Love. The Radicals, to tell the truth, place no soul in Gehenna, on account of their notion that, in reason, it does not exist, but also because, in their view, no justice could commit anyone to such a place. The Compromised, to tell the truth, have placed no soul in Gehenna on account of the notion that by revelation nothing has been shared concerning such a place; but they believe that justice should commit one to such a place.

You see how one renounces hope, while the other misconceives mercy, and, from it, misplaces and reshapes justice. Why not, with Balthasar, accept neither the assurance nor the certitude? Again, we the Weak, for our part, accept the existence of Gehenna, for that aspect of revelation is clear; and by that, we dismiss the Radicals' dismissal of Gehenna, but also their lie to will one's own good, as for another. And likewise, we admit, too, the admission of Gehenna by the Compromised, but not also the lie to will one's own good, as over another. The Radicals say in justice that it is known that even Cain, Judas, or Jericho's Ptolemy could not suffer Cocytus's ice; the Compromised say they could, but it is unknown, as revelation only exists for those in the heavenly sphere. The Weak say to each—to apply a notion of Love that neither party has yet uncovered—did not the mystic Catherine say that Love would annihilate such a place? And we add that as poles oppositely charged, one such nature cannot assume the other's privation.

The Radicals have not defined love. There is something of wisdom about that, but it does not save their view, which places love as an ethereal power bending to compromise, a power held to be too perfect for this world, but which, lacking substance, is formed as nothing more than the assumed true and good of any particular age. About the competing misconception, more will need to be said, for the Compromised have defined love; there is something of wisdom about that too, but to say, as Aquinas holds, reframing Aristotle's prior account, that, for the other's sake, love is to will the good for them, fails radically to resolve an ultimate impasse—that if a being is to be eternally separated from the Absolute, and only in the Absolute good exists, and there is no good outside of the Absolute, then, for an eternally damned being, no good can be willed, and thus the Absolute could not love the eternally damned. If this Absolute does not love all, nay cannot love all, then that defect, to the mind of the Weak, is insurmountable, and the Absolute ceases to be love. I desire to show you that this has been made clear; for it is my hope that you find our reasoning impeccable in its logic, and yet as one more instance that we, the Weak, are reasonable and our case acceptable for your consideration.

For you, dear Secretary, who personally hold few of our tenets, though you are included with eternal union in the eyes of the Radicals, who irrationally dismiss an eternally damned existence, you are not excluded from their love, in that, trying to contain everything, it becomes inclusive. But in calling no-things unloving, wrongly, they have called some-things dreadful as beautiful, making you unlovable; for in the union of the two, no good can be contained. And likewise, though excluded with eternal union in the eyes of the Compromised, who irrationally dismiss an eternally undamned existence, you are not excluded from their love in that, always trying to contain something, it becomes exclusive. But in calling some-things unloving, rightly, they have called some-things beautiful as dreadful making you unlovable; for in the union of the two, no good can be obtained. We love for the sake of our Friend, and neither for service nor fear. We hold that a Love union with the Absolute is your eternal future; and though it is by grace, we stress that the work of life is due, and of it, in this temporal state, remittance is disproportionately satisfied—that in and with our Friend, prior to eternity, rather there where it will compound exponentially, as by the worm which does not die and the fire is not quenched, you, I, and all, will be salted by fire; and salt is good, thus Love.

XLVIII

The Being of Love

I am writing to you this Lent, with the intention of this as the object of my fast; by today's liturgy, the Scrutinies are now past. So, in short, without elaboration, permit me to offer the Weak's definition of love, void of excessive development. Love is the origin of being, held as the created being's harmonic embodiment of the Absolute's self-attraction. It is that, in each of us, and in you also, Secretary; as this appurtenance, which is of the Absolute, though not the Absolute, remains that which flows back to the Absolute as source. Know that each idea of Being, as on our behalf, will be swept in by this current, harmonizing with other beings, with whom this idea of Being is equally shared; and in that one finds our cooperation. Attuned to the Absolute, the eternal Being joins our being with His. Further, as that which is of the Absolute but attuned to our nature, as always en route to return to the Absolute, the holy God-Head will not allow any individuation of this being, as a soul embedded with the idea of Love not to return in full union with the Absolute Being of its origin.

The contrivance of satisfaction, the method of its timeliness: these admittedly remain but a mystery to us. We fully confess that we know only partially. We do admit no conversion after death; but likewise, we have not settled on what constitutes this term we call death. Both the Radicals and Compromised, as with the culture at large, have evolved notions of death from heart to whole brain, from that of consciousness screening to undetectable rhythms, and from that of pyramidal cellular consciousness to consciousness timed-out. Has not the spirit of Love whispered to some of times past, as even in the previous covenant, and did not Leviticus Rabbah hand down to us the truth that for three days the soul, always near the body, seeks only to reunite. Furthermore, in the present, how ubiquitous are the accounts even from materialists, who know not whether to call the time between their so-called pronouncement of death to life's return, an after-life, or mere near-death, encounter. I do not question the content of their visions, but point out that, after they have been declared as having passed from this life, all that is evidenced as error by their so-called return is the inadequacy of the conceptualization of death as a failed measurement of the functions of each body. Let this stand as proof that, in that time when the body had seemed to escape death, it was but the soul which escaped detection.

So, then, in those days when the soul's state is on hold, imperceptible but attached to the body, as, together, forming the person, it is then that the deeds of the creature are enumerated, and in that time, the unimaginable pain of wrongs and omissions is laid bare. We, the Weak, hold that other created beings of our kind now passed, and beings eternally created for glory in the other realm, will, with the spirit of Love, minister to such recognition of the inescapable torment and pains we fell to in this life, caused by Love's privation. Our limited minds, lacking Love's presence at that time, might think that only annihilation could be capable of soothing such afflicted souls; but know, on that subject, that Love cannot, as the idea of Being, fall to eternal loss, nor disembark from existence by obliteration; for that is necessarily contrary to the nature of

Love and the idea of Being as our essence that each creates. Accept this, then, Secretary, as our hope and yours: that Love by mercy enters each heart and soul to assuage, now, what such an ultimate encounter certainly will bestow, that then a healing soul, as, in justice, each are made just, will, in the Absolute's sight, make those which were many now but one, engulfed in everlasting Love, being, now, home with the source of Love, each sharing eternal life with the Absolute as One.

XLIX

Neither Prediction nor Predication Can Resist Love

Some have said that those who find love do so while not ardently searching, while those who are in pursuit of love's pursuit do not find that which they seek; for each, then, the discovery of love was either found where it was not supposed to be, or the search for love constituted elements found in societal want. You see how each predicament presents love as an experience to be found by happenstance or in fortuity. Each is but a shadow of Love as the idea of Being.

Those scenarios presume, first, that love is set by terms of fulfillment, and, as properly predicted, once the satisfactions of those expected conditions are met, the anticipation now allayed is resolved, and love is thought realized as forecasted; or secondly, where such a view of love follows a desire, then, as determined by fulfillment, anticipatory expectations find solution in some epiphany of one's own prediction coming to pass in quite unlikely form. The mark of serendipity constitutes both experiences, where in each instance of the prediction of love or predication of love, the love which was found exceeded the love which was sought; either the love discovered exceeded expectations, or high expectations set a bar which was not reached. These are deficient understandings of Love, but yet both are quite beautiful, and, also, still stand as a testimony to love's power, in that love exceeds intolerance of substitutes or established measures nearer the ideal. Do you see that even among these earthly hurdles and obstacles, Love for the soul and souls remains an irresistible force?

Allow me, Secretary, to reflect again upon the nature of a thing, and use some analogies to show how the converse, exposed, often points to the truth; this is quite pertinent to the point at issue. Some have attempted to provide paradoxes to demonstrate absurdities; but they have unwittingly fallen into the disruption of natures as the unrecognized culprit, which, when demonstrated, suppresses the alleged conflict they intended to unveil. For example, though this was originally articulated elsewhere, Popper offered a paradox whereby a limitless tolerance would ultimately lead to the suppression of tolerance, meaning that which was once tolerated would be by some no longer tolerated, and thus the tolerant themselves would, paradoxically, become intolerant beings. What is the solution? First, this begs the question as to whether the nature of tolerance possesses the quality of absoluteness as essential; or should tolerance rather remain an endurance in the face of an opposition that has been first identified as evil or at least defective, held only until such time as it can be rectified? With the nature of tolerance restored, here by essential definition, then tolerance is always a resistance to an identified evil, and not an admission of laxness, which, as it wanes, becomes rigid.

Here is another example, adolescent, to be sure, but illustrative. An atheist argues that the omnipotency of the Absolute is absurd based on the purported conundrum that He could create a boulder too heavy to lift, limiting his omnipotence. Anthropomorphism aside, note this does not recognize the compound question fallacy, which is resolved by the fact that the term, "able to create a boulder too heavy to lift," is by nature poorly formed if such a thing cannot be created; while the term "unable to lift" no longer holds the same meaning if the boulder can be lifted. A thing only is, until it is not, and then it is no longer that thing. A boulder is too heavy to lift until it is not too heavy to lift. This concerns the nature of a thing; such intellectual nonsense clings to the a priori principle of non-contradiction as superfluous, in hopes of making a weak point appear strong. Returning from this analogy to that of Love, allow me to intertwine Love with a known physical law for comparison; the solution applies to both. If love is an irresistible force, and that irresistible force meets an immovable object—here, a person—then either the nature of love as an irresistible force is mistakenly held, or the person as the immovable object is, by nature, not that thing, and the former proposition is not true.

Love is an irresistible force, and no person's heart or mind is ultimately immovable. I hold it as uncontested that love seeks and finds its object. The target is the human mind and heart; then, whether exceeding predictions or finding its mark in ways not predicated, be this by happenstance or in fortuity, there is no indication in past history, nor in the present time, nor in any possible future, that when, in eternity, all time's raison d'être dissolves, the human person, always prepared like soft wax for the image of the seal, should be incapable of resisting the stamp of the Absolute's Love as form on human substance. Poetically put, "non vita, amore, morte ma piuttosto vita, morte, amore"; to paraphrase, the order is not life, love, then death, but rather life, death, then love. You see, there is but a single arrow that the Great Liar retains in his quiver, that is, to garble and warp the expectation and preparation of this idea of Love, so that, in our temporal frames, either love is thought found, and the quest culminates as an inferior form come to be held as authentic, or it is thought impossible, and therefore the quest is terminated as an inferior form which comes to be endorsed by satisfaction. Yet—and here the lie is undone—Love, as the idea of Being, was present by nature as essential to the human person. So neither predicting it not to be found, nor predicated as found where it was not supposed to be, each error places love as nonessential by nature. Love is of the Uncreated in the created, seeking the image and likeness of the Divine, by which the will and mind of man is to be yielded.

L

Repression of the Weak was Predicted

This deceitful technique, then, is the strategy; a single-sourced, twin assault on cultural distortion, in tandem with the deformation of the human person. A sinister blueprint indeed! For distorting the map does not require us to disfigure the territory. First remove the superior sense of the human person; once flattened to the material, the divine being is nothing else than the human being, said Feuerbach. As entirely plastic, what was undesirable has been shaved off. Courage has been whittled down to boldness, and honor is now sought as praise; those heroic virtues are among the casualties. The good life is then subverted; the wax is hardened and void of the bee's chosen nectar. The human person, as is falsely hoped, will not receive the form of Love: as one skews the potentiality, the actuality lies in waste.

In this way, the Radicals have captured the discourse; the earthly lecture halls are theirs. The typical commoner, as too good-natured, or out of a fear of being silenced in the public square, cedes the cultural bullhorn to the loud and proud, following what their concocted god has said; or, to put this another way, once the end is determined, they fashion a movement to conform. For the Compromised, it is less assuming but no less contagious, as morality becomes reduced to legality. They have captured the filter of revelation, and the earthly altars are theirs. Here the typical flock is too kindly disposed, or, out of fear of being silenced by the tribunal square, it cedes the clerical pulpit to the frock and finery, following what their contorted god has said;

or, to put this another way, once the end is determined, they fashion a canon to conform. Both want change, yet one asks only, "what should we want our god to do?" while the other asks only, "what could we want our god to do?" Neither are looking at the very thing our Friend asked of each of us; come, follow me, for if you are my disciples, then you are to love one another.

Though I realize that you hate him also, this is, as Solzhenitsyn predicted, because their seemingly benevolent concentration on social structures, coupled with a seemingly scientific approach, will be assumed to bear all defects of life, and will thus enter the minds of proles and flock by bullhorn and pulpit. Or, perhaps, since they are pressed into thinking, the veracity of their truth is determined by outrage, and deceit will be easily attuned to the desires of their grasping minds; it becomes a celebration of the *Culte de la Raison*, a glorious year-long eon under the guise of academic mottoes and designated jubilees. Oh, how these calculated campaigns work to repress the Weak! They chide, "we are up against the powers of the world"; as if either of them could be seen separated from such powers; Napoleon threatened Consalvi with destroying what our Friend has founded, only to be told the truth in taunt, that he will fare no better than those from within who have been trying to do so with no success.

The Weak claim that advanced victory, but find it scandalously arrogant to continue a charade in which movements and canons are thought the proper expressions of honor and courage. The Beloved Apostle spoke clearly to the effect that our Friend who shepherds us, said of His sheep that they hear His voice, and, being known by Him, follow Him. But recall, Secretary, that indeed sheep do hear the voice of their shepherd; note that when the sheep are ill, they do not recognize their shepherd's voice, and thus do not respond when called. The spirit of Love has clearly spoken, yet the Compromised and Radicals remain ill, and do not hear the voice of justice and Love. Whether it be the diseased culture or a person's ailing soul; we were warned that if those who cling to the world hate the Weak, we are to take comfort in knowing that our Friend was hated first.

LI

Our Friend's Work Magnifies Love

By being hated, we suffer; but to suffer is to rule, as to die is to rise. The work of our Friend has magnified Love's truth; and because of His work in the Weak, like yeast in a madre that spills over its container, the words we profess are not ours, but our Friend's, and do spill over into the world as truth and love; each which properly subsists alone in that form that images Him. But the world is His, as are those in it, so none are kept from our hope.

This life of our Lord and Friend, as the first to die and the first to rise, has borne the iniquities of all; so that, as all of our iniquities die in Him, we too will rise by Him. The gates of eternity opened by notice of His breath returned; where our Friend descended in search of the first Adam, and all the lost sheep who fell asleep redeemed only by the day when eternity entered time, those who, from the dawn of creation, came to life by our Friend. Then, which will surely come, on the day of days, our risen Friend will return once more in fully realized glory, with all the Absolute's created eternal beings, all balance and order returned, the work of the Adversary set aside, all solemnity ransomed, and ideologies grounded in episteme. Then all creation will blaze with Love revealed; with settled hearts, know majesty is with us.

LII

The Aberration of Nature Reveals Love

What will come in fullness, is now present as partial; the truth of love is found in the correction. No moral manual could contain that which guides us; like Tolkien's Quenya, the language of those immortal elves whose favor passed by the second age, such written moral wit no longer finds favor amongst us, common in heart and tongue, who seek guidance by the spirit of Love alone. Thus there is no formal moral standard in our practice of faith, but rather thoughts and acts are encircled by, and conform to, the love we proclaim. Let the Compromised keep their legalism, and the Radicals their relativism; for one it is attractive as being simple, to the other it is attractive as being benign. Can either satisfy the authentic needs of we who are human persons? What then is this guide of truth, other than adherence to a given nature that aligns with that which was written of our Friend while with us? What need could there be of rules to feed others, or for mandates to establish just societies? We use only what is needed, and if another is in hunger, we give them of our bread; and by so doing fulfill the precepts of the Compromised feeding of the poor, and by so doing satisfy the goals of the Radical's improved society. In what way are either separate?

As Day said, we must not only care for other's needs as far as we are immediately able, but we must try to build a better world; and we say it is enough to do so in that we see the other as ourselves. And, as the martyr King clearly pointed out, unlike the Priest who came upon a man, stripped and beaten, and, concerned only to maintain his own posture and status, just walked past, it was the Samaritan, an outsider, who asked only, if he did not stop, what would happen to the broken soul lying on the road? The Compromised have their postulations and the Radicals prioritize their actions, but we, the Weak, say theory and practice have no space between them. We seek only to become a living embodiment, an Icon of love that refracts the idea of Being, given to each as a return to the single point of our Omega. Neither aberration seems to realize the irony; nothing good in either deed, nor promise sprung from either the Sanhedrin or the Zealots at that time. Our Friend was accused of blasphemy by the former, but indeed, it was only He who acted by truth; and our Friend, as the hope of the Zealots, was but a shock to them when His love ushered in a Kingdom unrecognizable to their minds.

Let them say we do not follow their prescripts; let them say we do not plan to create their just societies; but also, Secretary, question them as to whether they see our Friend in the other, and so are asked, "when I was hungry, did you give me something to eat?" Will they respond, immediately and unreservedly, always and forever?

LIII

Enemies of Human Nature are an Oracle

I have pressed the distinctions between the two parties which rule over the Weak in numbers and by distinction. In this, our shared faith is set before us by the one Incarnate being, and to the Twelve who had been given Him. Those early disciples of our Friend were made enemies of their own kind, in the same manner as the current condition of the Weak. At that time, the powers of those adopted to culture despised them then as rigid bohemians; and the tradition from which they arose spurned their deviation from garnished exhibition. So do not doubt that then, as now, it was error which must, in logic, expose truth. Paul admonished us all that the gospel is the power of the Absolute for salvation, to everyone who has faith; in what way can truth be made plain if not by contrast? And further, to you, Great Secretary, such contrast must be discernible by the fact that an eternal power and deity, for the grace of our sake, is clearly perceived in the things which have been made. If this be true, then you, I, all are without excuse to admit that error is discoverable by our nature, and then, in that discovery, truth is made known.

Now what error has been exposed in discerning man's nature? Whenever such human interests have entered into conflict with immutable forms, the social kind was preferred over the natural. With Homer's gods and men now thoroughly mixed, then, by those minds, freedom was passed by law as Nyx and Hemera journeyed separately from each other; and as in fear, heeding the words of the Christian critic, they relinquished the perfect, since they thought it the enemy of the good. But in truth this phenomena erupts again in modern times, so, here, accept my litany: for from confusion arose the specialists, and in their tracks each discipline became isolated from the other. A pride of incompetence took hold of their minds; expert spoke to expert with little shared between them save their elevated specialty. And revealed faith was spurned for lack of proof; in the public square, the faith of secularism abounded. As though never grasping the supposition they held, they spurned the supernatural ends of humanity and all creation, with all the wit of Swift's "Big-Endians." In arenas of science and sociology, two became one, or perhaps five; self-reflective grievances couched in satire plucked at publications, but the jest fell flat; the universe, which is one, became many. Then gods became bigger than the universe, until the universe grew bigger than the gods.

Unmoored from nature, sperm became synthetic; the ovum was finally replicable; and with wombs then artificial, in the brave new world, the moral obliquity of childbearing became for culture not a pornographic impropriety, but a gross scatological savagery. It was overlooked that by undoing one aspect of nature, the others are necessarily undone; like Nestorius, denying the bearer of God the natural title God-Bearer, logic dictates that the God born with natures two, should become lessened to one. And as Huxley's fiction predicted with such engineered progeny, the words, "mother and father" have become obscene, on the premise that all language must be kept alive, never settled for acceptance, ever ready to conform to identity.

We stated that if thought can corrupt language, the converse is also true. Of this narrowing, in which all pleasure wipes out all pleasure, the Weak stand as an oracle to the boot forever stomping on the human face. Did not Swift also show that, as with the Houyhnhnms, authoritarianism is always spurned unless it is found attractive? In that case, it is supported. Such ideology survives only when dissent is deleted, yet surely thrives only when nature is nullified.

LIV

On the Origin of Conscience Tethered to Authenticity

Now with nature as what is discovered natural, authenticity assumes congruence to desire; but championed independence, to the blinded mind severed from the natural, is nothing more than an unconcealed conformity. Truth laughs at the scorn which falsity heaps upon it. The secular, and its two-front infiltration upon the Compromised and the Radicals, fail to fall upon the grace of our Friend; so we are awaiting the restoration to make us strong, established in His dominion alone. The Radicals speak of grace as a charism, but the supernatural source denied, the grace is evidence by merit of fellowship, thought to be abundant when the common measure is kept low; so they latch onto the partial truth of grace as inclusivity, but reduced to a value given to the postmodern spirit. Then grace, monetized by the Compromised, having become dispensers if not in substance, then by expression, for the hurdles of initiation once passed, they become merits won, and accomplishments are considered as now complete. They latch onto the partial truth of grace as exclusivity, but reduced to a value given to the accommodated spirit.

In response to both, then: grace is a non-thing, a space reduced. Consequently, it cannot increase as a battery to which the charge is restored, nor is it merely something that can be sourced from within; what measure, then, can signify what this grace is, and that this grace has reached its mark? If the Compromised speak of a grace necessary for earth's many troubles, then our gatherings become but a charging station; if the Radicals offer grace as nothing more than creative forces, then self-consistency is the only end. By neither account is proximity to our Friend the measure of this grace; and by it, then, perfection in reflecting the life given can never find, as the earthly sign, the human person elevated by the work of the spirit of Love.

Let it be clear, then, that the proper end of grace poured out is not truth lived as subjective authenticity; for then conscience is autonomy from any truth, be it sensed or self-imposed. This congruence and conformity, that Gramsci described as cultural hegemony, was to reduce the power of the Compromised, in concert with the so-called power minions of media, education, and family; and likewise then, in a pitiable irony, to the Radicals, who, by upholding his desire to close that gap left by Kant, would themselves become the very language of the master which served as the slogan of their revolt. Both lose some aspect of conscience and authenticity, and with it, alas, the experience of what this thing of grace is; each become poor agents of transformation. By the wisdom of Joan the Maid, our Friend must be first served; and then only by the grace of His friendship, measured solely by the closeness of the created to the Uncreated, will such origin of grace remain.

LV

Persecution and Injustice are Badges of Honor

You see then why, though we lament, what the Weak suffer is an earthly trophy. The victory is that we are quite aware of both the object of our scourging and the reasoning which has brought us to this point—unlike the conforming stillness of the Compromised, who are shielded from the truth, or those Radicals, with their aimless anarchism, who shield themselves from the truth. The former's sycophants allow nothing to reach the ears of the high and mighty, chauffeured by those they are called to serve; while the latter, with their "words and things," Scruton charges, place their truth with a nominalist sleight of hand, between inverted commas. We revolt for revealed and authentic truth, and, with mind and heart unshielded, tolerate persecution and injustice in the manner of our Friend, who, with his beard plucked out, found no shame.

The world is full of revolt; and though they are suppressed in academia, beauty, truth, and goodness remain those ideas defended with our breath and body. You have the seal that grants authority over the earthly powers of your jurisdiction; we have been awarded the seal which grants us powerlessness of the domain we call, "the already, but not yet." The cross, the low form of death conquered by One, has been given to us in minutia, so that we may, by His honor, be made high. Now, you asked where you find the Weak, would you find the spirit of Love; we say where you find the spirit of Love, may you there too find the Weak. By grace, may we stand true in our love, and know that, wherever there is true love, "Deus ibi es," God is there.

LVI

The Appearance of Means and Reform

Oh, what promises can be made with angelic oration and sophistic script! But their words wither hearts, and cast mountains of men into the sea. All compassion is attached to the intention of their speech and writing, but the object is of another sort. And if their spiritual canons and liberal legislation result in injustices and the reputational deaths of hundreds, what is it to them? For they intended good. They pick a powerless scoundrel for their sacrifice, and, once forced to terms of nondisclosure, or headlines controlled by media-fed diets, they think they have sold a pearl to the public, with arguments that it was formed by them, as the oyster. In reality, they are the oysters, but the Weak became the sand which was formed as the irritation brought to their unveiled enterprises; with their sins against prudence and justice, such reasoned deception earns them their eight-tiered Malebolge residence. As for them such social and political reform is overbilled to society as a whole, while their individual reform was undersold to the whole of society, who trusted that their purposes were good. Their theological agitations and political schisms wall them in with ten rocky circular valleys, serving merely as the setting for Virgil's ride upon a monster.

LVII

The Philosopher Foretold Societal Demise

The famous ways of the Borgia have been pressed subtly into more recent covert machinations of moral treachery. This tests the Liar's pride, by not granting direct recognition; and with such worldly infiltrations, the masses have grown weary of seeing justice and rights subverted by the caused divisions and eminent floundering of the Compromised and Radicals. They employ the same means as secular profit seekers, but under the cloak of the crucifix or fist and rose. Yet this falling short, particularly when notoriously witnessed, is illogically weaponized to make the recognizable defect signify the death of revealed truth. If Lenin's oft-repeated ineffective defense, proffered by those amenable to his prose, is to claim that his system is not wrong, but has not been tried properly, why, then, is that fiendishly concocted slogan not afforded theistic movements with equal charity? Or pressing this further, even the Way which we claim as right and just is often not tried well by other progeny, who seek their own notoriety.

Our theistic enterprise is admittedly wounded by many, but secular malevolence tastes no sweeter simply because it admits only a temporal goal. This exposing appraisal of our Friend's heritage forms as a result of vice. That is easy enough to claim, as they aim at seeking the profit and the spirit of scheming men, rather than the gain from Love of the Absolute. Recall that Borgia courted Machiavelli, who maintained two moral spheres, where cruelty was thought of as mercy, and it showed; and Bordiga, who insisted that the petty bourgeoisie was mere opportunists, boasted that he was more Leninist than Lenin, and this, too, showed. Such contrasting societal issues even the Philosopher could not reconcile, as was his gift. But the Philosopher did warn that, as was the case with both Borgia and Bordiga, if a person is driven to be a means to an end, as with the Compromised, or disproportionate corrective gratuities are enforced, as with the Radicals, a resentment of law would surface; and it did. It has manifested both in our sects and that too of the State; each as the tearing of a right from a nature.

The creation of human rights should boast no origin in the State; rights precede the State, save the well-being of those to whom the Absolute has entrusted custody. But you see that this too relies on a nature; for as the right is connected to a good, the good must retain something essential for the good to form. What has occurred, for both Machiavelli and Lenin, is that the good is thought to be formed in two ways. The first way is by experience, which cannot be disregarded, but neither can it become the prime value of a phenomenon. For when one reduces the phenomena to an experience—to use as an example; "I fear water, and hold that as objective"—only a shared expression of those who also fear water will be thought worthy to validate it. In such a case what is essential, is subverted by the accidental. But secondly, if the nature can be nothing more than the explanation of that thing in terms of scientific criteria, holding only to a shared expression with those who accept only that which is empirically verifiable—to continue with our example, "water is a compound"—this leads no one closer to the nature of the thing. It proposes, perhaps, something mind-independent, but what is essential becomes subverted by the physical. For example, to consider water further; it is experienced subjectively for how it tastes, erodes, and soaks; but when reduced physically to the compound of hydrogen and oxygen, neither tasting, eroding, or soaking comes to mind. The reduction does not match the experience; no one tastes hydrogen and oxygen. I am not addressing here the centuries-old metaphysical water debate; I mention it only because you have commented on it in your publications; yet I do affirm that what is commonly known as water behaves as expected and forms what some may call a law-like nature.

The point is that the prediction of tasting, eroding, and soaking, flows from the law-like nature of water. As to the first error, the subjective experience squeezes the nature into a little truth; and as to the second error, the reduction to the physical squeezes the nature into a proposition which is only a little truthful. Now, applying this to the decline of society, what good can be essentially tethered to the subjective "little truth" or the reduced "little-truthful," save that which compels the powers of the status quo to choose the necessary moral sphere or class opportunism, as a means to wedge their own good into the space their fragmentary truth has prepared? This is crafty totalitarianism, and the vehicle for their goals is the vitiation of human nature. As in all things, the societal demise begins in and with the individual person; for society is, collectively, but each person writ large. On this the Philosopher is clear: rights remain invested in persons; persons are determined by their nature; from these rights by nature arise legal duties which preserve moral boundaries. This both respects the faculty of self and others; and in its absence, society forms only around those fractional truths that produce moral hazards, and which, in parasitic fashion, twist human nature. This process culminates in the submission of each person individually, and the capitulation of society as a whole collectively. The human person is the zenith of creation; and the created Liar remains an apex predator.

LVIII

Culprits of Contemporary Aspirations

The subtlety of these designs is cunning. In contemporary society, it has resulted in a public moral lobotomy; with insult to injury, the lobotomized leaders of the Compromised and Radicals aspire to be society's physicians. How does this progress? With narcissistic skill they flatter others, and by increasing the notoriety of their circles of friends, they hope to be equally boosted, as they then share in their friends' notoriety. Two unscrupulous ends are met; the friends become endeared to the flatterer, and the flatterer, in return, is garlanded with high praise by the friends who stoke their ego with the same intent. This they share between them, each too grandiose in their own egos to identify the malignant pathology which disables them all.

The Compromised leaders are counseled by parrots; the speechless echoes parade, as their lackey-mirrors reflect the views of their beholders. The Radical leaders celebrate the cohorts who, in a swarm, envelope them within their think-circles; the Saussurean self-reflectors use their arbitrary words to speak capricious truth to their sage on stage. These puffed-up egos self-inflate: the Compromised pervert Aristotle's friendship of utility into one held close for the subservient derivatives it produces, while the Radicals distort friendship as a foible for pleasure, maintaining the relation by degree until their interests are served.

We, the Weak, speak neither of the goodness of the consequences nor the goodness of the pleasure, but of goodness as excellence, defined by Him who first loved us. We seek the third as a good, as outside the two, traversing both needs and value in an asymmetrical reciprocity. The potential space between giver and giver is filled by the Love given. Heresy reassembles this relation, and, by attractive plots, yields to the adoption of lesser goods to occupy that voided third. In the same way, when tempted in the desert, our Friend was lured by three of the Liar's offers: to enjoy a vulgar display of satisfaction; to summon forces gratifying the ego; and to adore the created with power as the prize. These stately seductions are primers for the forces that bear down on our earthly friendships, both with each other, and with our Friend. The first baits power for the glamour of its gratifying use, the second with gratified ego turns to captivate the charms of pleasure; and in the final perversion the pleasure of the created inverses love reserved solely for the Uncreated.

So that as a warning to us, the Weak, even the Icon can be idolized if proper ends are reversed; and when status of advantage and approval are appraised for the display of utility and pleasure, the contemporary culprit is unveiled. We swear only to resist while in the desert, by our Friend's grace resisting, until His promise is fulfilled, remaining on our earthly pilgrimage, boasting only the image of the Absolute, who, for us, is this idea of Love.

LIX

How the Philosopher is Tethered to Love

Now I will tell you of this idea of Love, given to each but not from each, as an undetermined gift of the Creator to the created. The Philosopher spoke of the idea of Being; you are well acquainted with his proposal. Did not Plotinus grant Love's birth from Poverty, seeking what is noble and unchangeable? What can be immutable, save that which does not decay? And from that the quest for all ideas forms, from but one, necessarily; as a candle contingent on a flame not of its own. Even Heidegger held it as axiomatic to determine that which must be held as being, in order to hold that which is determinable; this Love as Being comes not from sense, but is aroused by sense forms as determined.

This, as a last abstraction, even the Philosopher did not explicitly call Love. Though not admitted as either pure mental construct or of an eminent deity conferred to all reality, this Idea as Love, like the Absolute who is Love, finds residence in mankind as the precedence for Love. It is not the Absolute itself, but this Love is of the Absolute. If this seems to be theory in excess, and lacking requisite coherence, the speculative is not always a substitute for the inept, for Picasso expressed the abstract as an utterance of vision and not from any lack of expertise. Therefore I beg you to not dismiss such originality, for many things in reality are less true, yet are thought true simply because they are more readily comprehensible. Noble truths and long-sufferance are twinned deities often found in want, but whose esteem lies in the depth of their treasure. Though this, as a complex thought, is not to be conflated with convoluted jargon, also let not its lengthy presentation be thought erroneous merely because terse oversimplification is perceived as true by virtue of rapid discernment.

LX

How the Philosopher is Tethered to Sacrifice

Now consider Julian again. He usurped the hierarchy, and, by his inverted worship sought to rehabilitate this relation of man and gods, though he did expose at least the necessity for sacrifice. To the Weak, this thing of the self as one, granted to another, and inclined to all finds solace of Being only when, as the indeterminate appurtenance as Idea, it is aroused; then does this gift diffuse as prepared in reception as other shared beings of this Idea; who also with this Idea, receives that which does not originate in either, but which is ultimately drawn to the shared Origin. This is the Absolute's self-attraction, a Deity calling Deity to self, and communicated by the spirit of Love. Where Creator and creature are united and drawn on by His will, this union with our will enters others; and in others Him, and in Him, ours. This Love as an idea of Being, perpetual in motion, is a liturgy of wills, with powers not yet failed by imagination. Where will and desire are balanced, we are granted a glimpse of eternal states; while in this temporal existence we are given to each other, as our Friend had given Himself to us, and thus we propagate liturgical living.

To love is not by necessity to sacrifice, because love and sacrifice stand singly together, by dimensions of their own. This is why we speak of receiving only in terms of giving: the dichotomy is resolved by the gain appearing as loss, but what is granted to one, is granted to all. As the Uncreated hand moves the sun and other stars, the created hand loses nothing by that enterprise;

in fact, it gains all. In Moore's phrase, "all that was sweet was made but to be lost only when so sweet"; for the Weak, it is only when this gain appears to be lost, that both love and Love, do in truth sweetly meet.

LXI

The Natural Signifies the Spiritual

Such passivity is thought to be in this love and those wills; which I suspect you discern, but you need to know that this does not disrupt the lack of intention. Cicero spoke of planting trees which will be used in another age, and to such selfless forethought we attribute wisdom and love; but do not many mighty trees, by root or seed proliferate without willful aid, and the shade from each then become a benefit to those who seek refuge under it, regardless of whether the tree has been planted or permitted to mature? The argument that there is no intention here, whether to plant or permit, dismisses the Absolute, who, either by the idea of Being or by natural propagation, would not have the same spirit of Love endeavor both as origin. Permit me here to explore the role of intention in relation to Love and the Absolute.

So as to manifest an unseen reality, our Friend has inaugurated signs for our initiation, and thus for us is given a Three-Fold spiritual cleansing. But we offer it to the new-born, which some consider illicit, for they claim that this expresses no intention. I refer you back to the shade and refuge analogy: the instantiation of this idea of Being is without favor, as the one who plants by intent, will find no advantage over those who propagate what by nature spread. So, we immerse in water those who, with no seeming choice, differ only by age from those who, though they have expressed a desire for it, were simply submitting naturally to that which is offered to all. To our understanding, neither sacrifice nor love is a choice, though each can be desired; then, in similar fashion, the response to sacrifice and love can be given when it is desirable to nature, yet not explicitly expressed. As the water cleanses and nourishes, know too that it destroys with a fury no other natural power can muster; those will-swept passions are rushed on like loose twigs by its current.

Then just as the Holy Voice revealed to all that "this is my Holy Son," so too our young are crowned with steadfast love and mercy by the same voice now spoken in the water. Thus they are plunged into His death as sacrifice, and are so consummated by His resurrection as love for the world, that both those young and old are raised with Him. Now, when our Friend revived Adam in earthly form, nature was redeemed; that which had been invisible was made visible; what had been distorted was restored. This is not to hold, that there are not those who reflect Him more fully; for as declared by Esaias, that which is scarlet is made white like wool; but this is given to all who are illuminated by the spirit of Love. Yet do not parents seek the privileges and rights of citizenship for their children from birth? When the benefits of state are chosen not by them, but on their behalf, what of those individuals who seem passive, and express no intention? Is it not accepted that the sacrifice of our Friend, the power of the spirit of Love, and the will of the Absolute call them to the water as citizens of eternity, and that this is the only intention needed? So too, with this Love as the idea of Being, which, as given to all, and explicitly recognized by some, is not predicated on the intent of the created, but the intended will of the Uncreated.

Secretary, I beg that you seek shade under the trees our Friend has planted; so that you may find these words I now offer not just reasonable, but capable of being acted on too, by His Love to transform the will and mind through a power no resistance can defy.

LXII

How Culture Imitates Love as Conformity

What then holds you back from this journey? What imitation is set before you and others, substituting such a ritual for the superfluous, of this world set as self-determined, and satisfied with technological wonders which past generations would think possible only through magic? You seek reason, and, from such wisdom, the hope that this god will bring you peace; but you will find only the destruction of the peace you seek. I say that even Zeus desired peace, and, though thought to be wise, he became enraged as Aphrodite, borne of sea foam and sky, who brought to Troy destruction by seduction. This world's present lot will suffer nothing different if collective privileges and social reforms are not countenanced; conforming to the forms of the privileged, these hoped-for social corrections will be eviscerated. Diversity is thought to be under siege, yet the antidote remains for honor and courage to be retrieved.

All act as though this privilege and reform are self-directing means; but used as ends in themselves, they seek only continuous refinement not as errors peeled away, but perpetual coats of color applied to appease the current fashions. For example, in times of strife and uncertainty, basic needs and development are sought; whereas in times of satisfaction, the accidental becomes mistaken for the essential. By analogy, a homeowner seeks to alleviate major disrepairs, and does not tolerate unreliable mechanicals or a crumbling foundation, finding either worthy of immediate attention; so repairs are sought, to return the home to a habitable condition. But as often is the case, when such basic needs are satisfied, the homeowner turns to their wants; out of a fidgety compulsion, they update appliances and furniture merely for aesthetic reasons; and for convenience's sake, they enlarge their living spaces under the pretense of necessity for entertaining friends. Then art is hung not to be appreciated, but to adorn their egos; and glasses and books are spontaneously aligned to impress those who come to visit what they call not a home but a house. So, too, this is replicated in society. With the basics of care and shelter satisfied, injustices are then sought out, often rightly so; but then, in like manner, to satisfy the egos of one and many, social equity is cultivated, and inclusion, whatever those terms might mean to the merchants of such terms, become the aesthetics of the elite's societal house.

This is good, you might say; and perhaps it is; but it points to the many justices achieved in one's country house, or there would be no polishing of brass lamps and porcelain vases. This makes sense only to those who, ironically, are privileged to afford such leisure time and fresh-cut flora. Oliver Twist did not seek redress for fashion and identity, but desired to reduce the limitations of hunger and his disadvantaged station. Yet the nobles of society, Compromised and Radicals both, with their concern for lamps and vases, fail to contend that honoring progressive improvement is only placated if one has the means; and that such nuanced societal tuning is found excessive and unwanted by those whose concern is but for adequate health and consistent income. People become projects. This, the Compromised say, is their mission to serve, and the

Radicals say that this is their mission to rectify; but neither have the courage for such change, since they lack the necessary fortitude required for the task themselves. Each is content with giving Twist only the idea of soup, and, in so doing, they merely pamper their own egos. Do you agree that this is but unrecognized conformity, that they indulge the vices thought to be virtues, then extol others to their virtues that by conformity, oblige actions to form vices? They think themselves trend setters, but are little more than trend seekers; each respectfully indulges their accumulated luxuries and stacked-up privileges, while denouncing the scant-held luxuries and pint-sized privileges of others. The leaders of the Compromised reside in their mansions, while the Weak are scorned for not affirming such use as a necessary accommodation of their status; the leaders of the Radicals tap on devices they denounce, made by their own market demands, yet they scour the Weak for not affirming such use as a necessary accommodation of their reform.

For the Compromised, privilege is the sign of blessing; for the Radicals, privilege is the sign of a curse; the first thinks how right we are, the second thinks how wrong they are. For the first, they say, "look at what has been granted us"; for the second, they say, "look at what has not been granted others"; but notice that, in each instance, they do not look at what they themselves possess, or here do not possess, particularly the failure to cultivate either honor or courage, which, ironically, can alter the privileges they themselves hold, or the privileges they deny, if such denial suits their goal. This is not to make light of the injustices that are embedded in privilege and may be alleviated by reforms, but each error finds comfort in such privilege in converse ways, while both claim to fight a single injustice. If one accepts that to some degree injustice may secure resilience, it is to the fullest degree that comfort only breeds contempt. The masses of both the Compromised and Radicals are encouraged to seek political and social reform, while laughably unable to muster the virtues necessary to accomplish either. Far worse are the efforts they put forth deceitfully for intended displays of love; you must know that this is not their ultimate goal. Menelaus went to war under the guise of retrieving Helen, but his sights were set on Troy from the outset, only feigning that his hope rested solely in recapturing her fair countenance.

The Weak exhort you, Dear Secretary, to move beyond this misguided single-mindedness, because those who speak of reform, intend only control. If you seek peace, seek it at the expense of genuine injustices, from the hands of the temperamental performers and those cultural hemophiliacs, and not in the ruin of those of the Weak you think are disruptors. Rather, condition yourself to overcome your own deficit: as Helen hid in Egypt, so too does inequity and exclusion reside in places not readily considered, for congruity to overabundance is only harmony with fashions. Conformity and tolerance are not agents of love, but poor substitutes; for in virtues shared by creature and Creator, whose love alone outweighs all vice, seek justice, and you will be at peace; be just, and then you will grant peace to others.

LXIII

The Absolute Revealed and Heresy Exhumed

With the twinned division like a curtain torn in two, now that the veil is parted, and misrepresentation exposed, the created's moral infinite is found to be the Absolute's eternal ideal. The Philosopher, who first proposed this endless Being, holds that it moves from perfection to light, and discovers such a Cause, everlasting in law and virtue, as the Absolute Being, knowable by light and reason. In harmonic fashion, the human person partakes of the infinite by uniting to the Idea of infinite value, as other, in other beings; this is the long-searched-for rational theology to be found in the cosmos. The Absolute spilled into man; and in right society, where the goals of each met collectively, each ideal in man is shared by the Absolute, as each ideal being is in accord with endless Being, neither equivocal nor univocal. For man is not known without the body given, yet, by Him, is known as Being in itself.

This is how the Absolute revealed such a pursuit of knowledge to the Philosopher, though it appears as obscure words by an obscure Philosopher. Recall that it was once quipped, by Kissinger in fact, that to be well-known affords the benefit, to the extent one is misunderstood, that such misunderstanding falls as a mark of deficiency in the reader and not the writer of the words. I am neither such a philosopher nor a recognized statesman, but I pray any dimness found in my synopsis which is contained within this report, be so inversely greater to my own lack of prominence and skill of pen that it be remembered, and not me. Know, then, that the sublime solicits intricate elaborations; vile simplicity finds solace in unsophisticated expression. Therefore errors are more easily phrased, more easily disguised, and thus more readily digested, when the point is deviously plain. For example, redemption is, for some, a truth marketed only as snow-covered heaps of dung. As for us, the Weak, given such knowledge by the Philosopher, we contend with heretical shortcomings from times past, whose piled excrement, abundantly found and likewise easily deposited, and coated by sinister speech, suffers the present stench only with thin-shelled logic; it is but broken.

As it was from the bowels of the Liar that Nestorius and Marcion issued forth, so with no less heavy heart do we profess that Borgia and Bernays crawled about with equal worldly charm, under a guise thought to be full of wit. The one brought Renaissance delight to the Compromised's throne, while the other cloaked his uncle's spells for the Radical's stool; each think themselves so distant from the compost which nourished their festered missions, and which gave rankness to their voice. Yet what were fed to their unsuspecting admirers were but the digested twinned-covert defects of enlightenment and progress; and then, once distant from its introduction, each subsequent generation becomes accustomed to it, as an ever reappearing two-eyed feng, the aberration becomes accepted as tradition.

LXIV

Misrepresentations, Falsehoods, and Reality of Persons

I will speak further, though I fear to overburden your by-now weary heart and mind, before I proceed to conclude with good news, which, in hope, undoes the distress such stated truths most assuredly induce. So then, in trepidation, allow me, the lowest of the Weak, to provoke in this one last brief space, words that, if you had given me your ear directly, would be inescapable realities from my lips. So that you do not excuse the machinations of the Compromised and Radicals presented as solitary aberrations, consider whose seeds they have planted in their gardens, and how an error, once minute in origin and sweet to the ears of one who desires compassion, finds a divergent path later, once accepted—growing to such a great distance from its point of departure that those who boast themselves on the right side of history will erroneously encamp outside truth's narrow gate within a half century.

Truth is not contained entirely within a definition, but a definition does both preserve some of what the truth contains and excludes some of what it does not; and points to how these beings which we are as persons, are thwarted when experience misaligns with contained truth and excludes reality. Each attempts to preserve one aspect of a truth at the expense of the other aspect of truth, which is necessary to its nature. For example, Nestorius, who preferred a loose binding of our Friend's natures, did so to preserve the eternalness of the Absolute from the temporality of our Friend, and in the wake of this preference, the Incarnation and our God-Bearer would have been swiped away with one evil error. His lie formed a claim that only like natures issue forth from like natures; and from that, he who died could not be He who does not die. In a similar perverse admiration, Borgia divided the everlasting from the decayable, in an attempt to preserve what can be sensed as pleasurable, with naked courtesans and chestnuts under creeping knee; He who is Unseen was worn but as a cloak. And even if by slight calumny such a reputation has been gained, both common folk and intellectuals accept it as such from the diary set forth. In this splitting of the temporal and eternal natures, and thus denying as a sign each incarnate nature given to man—and the death our truth witnesses too—only the loss of temporal goods remains. So now to Marcion, who, rather than dividing our Friend in two, preferred a higher god to explain theodicy and a lesser one to be given as our Friend; to think that on the tree was sacrificed the lower one, and that this Man, our visible Friend, was but an apparition of the invisible Absolute. This by analogous like-minded weakness. And now to Bernays, who, denying the higher nature of which man partakes, entreats the lower nature, with its appetites sought as fetters for propaganda. Public opinion is crystallized, and those invisible powers gained to rule the visible masses: in each, producers of desire prevail, as that which dons the cap of lesser goods. What else could this claim be, for all such fornicators of truth, but to affirm with heart and mind that two plus two is five? You could hear that claim from Oceania, as waves pounding the shores: freedom is slavery; ignorance is strength; war is peace. It rolls in; carrying with it a deceit not so easily detected, festering in the corners of generational hearts. From these past truths—now inverted, and preset for present control—lies sold as such could never reach so many, so easily, so deeply as in the days of old. Such falsehoods are called real because the experience is instilled; then, as the lie confirms the experience; thus the falsehood is accepted.

Experiences, dear Secretary, are not properly exportable; only the Love we claim can resolve the discrepancy; allow me to explicate further how lies experienced become false truths affirmed. If someone speaks of being afraid, or cold, the response cannot be, "you are not afraid," or "you are not cold." You may ask about the sufficient conditions of being presently safe or warm, but flatly to deny their experience is thought dismissive of the person; and thus love did not prevail on the part of the speaker who did not share that experience. The same then applies to claims of offense. If it is reported that one's speech or text offends another, the dialogue cannot ensue by simply making the claim that it does not offend; though one may present the conditions as either misunderstood, exaggerated, or lacking a rational basis to cause offense, but to flatly deny their offense is thought dismissive of the person; and thus, in this regard, love did not prevail on the part of the listener who did not share that experience. For each, the dismissal of personhood was attached to perception, and perception is tethered to a non-exportable experience. Though each may be necessary, in the end neither is a sufficient condition for love, which is experienced, but which is not reducible to the subjective; or else power wielded by forced falsehoods or misrepresentations would prevail.

The immutable nature of truths—here love and personhood—like middle terms, must soundly link commonality to those minor and major premises I have offered, resulting in a conclusion soundly capable of conveying reality; that is, as a triumph of love predicated of truth. I will write no more on this; but I will now speak to the triumph of courage and honor; as, for both you and me, by them the hope of our spirit of Love, which exceeds our minds, could now swell in our hearts, as a real experience for all of our nature we call person.

LXV

The Form of Our Signs

Allow light now to overtake your darkness. For today, on this very day I write, the only day, upon which there is no sacrifice of our Friend, we proclaim that through the cross you brought joy to the world. Those who are illuminated come to our table prepared; those who wish to be among us seek initiation in our presence. Take note, I speak of our table and our presence, even in my bodily absence. And with this liturgy, our prayer; we pray to receive those called Elect.

To their formation, in weeks past, the first pericope has been put to them: the woman at the well, whom our Friend searched out by name, Mary, was given living water, and so too will the elect. Like the God-Bearer, our Friend embraced her as woman, because she asked for the water of life. She went from being a Samaritan to following our Friend: darkness to light, she was welcomed into His fellowship.

The second pericope is put to them whom our Friend met prior to entering the Temple: squatting to meet the lowly blind man, then with spittle mixed with mud. He went from being a beggar to a seer transformed, since, with such faith expressed, he believed in our Friend as the Son of Man: darkness to light, restricted from Temple entry no more.

The final pericope is put to them. Our Friend travels to Bethany for the raising of the man called Lazarus. Dead for three days, our Friend commands him to come out; he is now arisen, bandages removed, and dignity restored: darkness to light, returned to the community whole.

The elect are then told: "you are the woman at the well reformed, ask for baptism"; "you are the man with sight restored, ask to be anointed"; "you are Lazarus who was raised, ask to eat His flesh and drink His blood." This same Friend, doing the work of the Absolute, in the power of the spirit of Love, He who called the Samaritan woman to fellowship, now calls you to baptism; He who called the man born blind to enter the Temple, now calls on you to confirm the same faith; He who raised Lazarus from the dead, now calls you to the table of new life. No one is to be excluded from the cleansing bath who seeks; no one is to be excluded from the anointing who seeks; no one is to be excluded from the table of new life who seeks.

And though the command is phrased in this way—"ask and it will be given"; "seek and it shall be found"—know that this is no initiative of the creature's. For though I said "all who seek"; it is all with Love implanted in Being, only that Love seeks Love. Nietzsche's madman shouting in the marketplace, "I seek God," should not be scorned on account of the killing of God, as so indifferently placed in such joyous science of a cavalier dismissal; rather it is Love asking, and Love given; Love sought, and Love found. But if you persist in questioning, to whom should it be given, save to those who ask; and who would ask, if first they did not seek? I put to you what transpired between our Friend's entry into Jerusalem and His entry into the grave; for at that time, there were those, like the Compromised, who preserved their Temple lives, and those of that time like the Radicals, who shouted for Barabbas; it was neither Jerusalem nor the grave who chose our Friend. By sole initiation was His will brought to bear on that which was to receive such form; and both the Temple life and Barabbas's revolt were but privations of our Friend's Love.

Only of human love, does such love seek human merit; recall the poem which the Hound of Heaven orates: "Ah, fondest, blindest, weakest, I am He whom thou seekest." From darkness to light, the spirit of Love forms our signs; it is the water that cleanses, sustains, and destroys; the oil that approves and soothes as balm; it is the Bread given as wheat and the Wine given as grape that become for us sustenance and inebriation; of this Love which first chose us.

LXVI

The Sign of the Resurrection

The food and drink of everlasting life is the taste of our resurrection; and our Friend will certainly raise up those who call to Him; for we do become that which we eat and drink. But realize that His friendship is a proposal that is given, and those to whom He offers may freely take. The manna in the desert was given by the Absolute to His people being formed, and they grumbled; the crowds asked our Friend for a sign, and He offered Himself to them as the Bread of Love; yet responding, they said to Him, Lord, give us this bread always; and He said in reply, "Who comes to me I will not cast out."

To you, Secretary, I say: that is the Bread of Eternity, given in the words of spirit and life. Only those that the Absolute grants come to Him; but, take note, not in any instance did our Friend press anyone to accept Him as the Bread and Wine; and take note also that in any instance when someone asked our Friend for the heavenly food, they were given Him. You have asked, how can this be that the flesh and blood of our Friend, long ascended from this earth, be the Bread and Wine we eat and drink as the sign of resurrection? It is enough that one says; "Amen, it is Him," and then it is given. If you think it too effortless, and rather elementary to affirm; "Amen, it is Him," then seek metaphysical explanations; you may do so; but there are some mysteries that such temporal minds cannot contain. If you think that my attempt to bypass proof of our assurance, in return for the Weak I represent, I ask, what proof would suffice?

Others have tried; the God of the Compromised is made too big for the universe, and entities, said Ockham, should not be multiplied unnecessarily, as they sometimes are in proofs; alternately, the universe of the Radicals is made too big for their god, and language, said Derrida, is dispossessed of longed-for presence in any attempt to seize it, as they sometimes do in disproofs.

So, what we do in remembrance of Him, we do; that is enough. For it is He, and as no proof would suffice to demonstrate that our Friend was both God and Man, no proof will suffice to demonstrate that our Friend is both Bread and Wine. It can be explained, but to what end, save that we would be vindicated, and you would disapprove on material principle. What the Liar tends to sow, is not disproof but doubt; we the Weak reside in the degrees between the claims of metaphysics and physics. As He said, "I am," we say, "He is"; and as He said, "This is my Body and Blood," we say, "It is He." You must remove all doubt.

LXVII

The Form of Our Service

Now those who are counted among us, are those of the Friend to whom the Absolute called, and those that accepted as invitation the restoration from darkness to light, when the weekly possibility is afforded for us to gather in one place, without respect for position or persons; for among the Weak, little wealth persists, the designated home becomes our home. As the Weak are scattered, like wheat harvested to be threshed, and grapes picked to be trampled, we assemble accordingly, of the region where present, on the day that He rose; gathered together, in polyphonic voice with candles lit, we enter the assembly as one Body, where word and meal will nourish us in fellowship and service. From among us, the Servant whom the spirit of Love has chosen, moves to the fore; if there is a stranger in our gathering, let them be afforded the place of honor. All gaze and face the image that moves with us in pilgrimage: the Icon, unfurled for our veneration. In this, we celebrate creation and redemption. First, for our own faults, we respond: our sins are many, but your mercy is greater. Then, giving glory to our Friend who has taken away these faults, one among us reads from the writings preserved by the faithful, which, accordingly our Servant follows by proclaiming from the Apostle's testimonies, that which came to Israel first, and is now fulfilled by our Friend; to our life and stations he or another relates such good news. As the creed by which we have striven to live is proclaimed, from the many, we are made one Body. Then those gifts of bread, wine, and water, that have been prepared by created nature, as procured by the community, are brought forth; now at our Servant's outstretched hands they become prepared by the nature of the Uncreated. An antiphon is recited by all; then, with hearts and minds lifted up, the Servant becomes lower. First, the linen yoke is placed on his shoulders. With weighted hem, the sackcloth is draped across the neck, ever to caution that in his identity, it is the burden of the faithful that they must bear to lighten; then, with ministers standing upon each side, the Servant is veiled from the assembly with the shroud of the saints. At this time, only voice reveals his posture, for thanks and praise is then given to the Absolute as never ceasing to restore the covenants we have broken; and now He offers us this final bond, that not even death can render us from His Love. We chant the holy praises; the Servant prays according to ability; we respond; "Death destroyed death, Life restored life; come to us, and with us always be." Then, to reverse the traitor's kiss, we share that peace which our Friend has freely given, one to another with both lips and embrace. Let our reconciliation not be in vain. As given gifts, the water from His side mingles with the wine, and both, with bread, are lifted to become our happy supper. Our "Amen" is our consent. From the preceding joy and sorrow that accompany our lives, united to this Bread and Wine, and given to Him; participation by us makes this sacrifice His and ours. All whom our Friend has chosen, and who are now reconciled to be present among us, are given portions of the Bread and Wine, as with and through our Friend, our Body and Blood. And for our journey and provision, and to all those distant and present, this Bread is taken as spare meals: in this we all are made one in Him. This is everlasting life; our hearts move from darkness to light; our spirits rejoice. Some from each is collected; the faithful carry what all have to offer, with a portion of the Bread for those either old or ill; so that our precarity is always present, such is given in entirety to those of our community who live beneath dignity afforded our form. All who are in need of sustenance and restoration have been brought to prayer, for with us all faithful are united in and by the spirit of Love.

LXVIII
Conclusion

Accept or decline, adopt or refute, but do not remain indifferent to this plea. You are not outside of the Absolute's province, and will stand condemned or resolved to the extent that you either concur or show resolve to the Weak. May the light of our Friend rising in glory dispel the darkness of my heart and mind, and so too with yours, Dear Secretary! I see eternity through the window slit, and find solace in that Love, which is better than life; with whom I will soon be one; I plead that you insistently place faith in my intentions, and not solely on the eyes whose gaze finds rest on these pages. If our Friend responded to Pilate, "I am," then allow me, please, in grace, only to say, "I am only what I am." I pray that my creativity does not stem from such obscure sources; not to match your acumen, acclaimed by East and West.

This is offered as my sole proposal; I make no attempt to merge it with other reports; an artist provides vision, and though it is said that two minds are greater than one, the compromise of two visions produces a third inferior to each. So, on what has been given, I shall stand or fall; unlike the Radicals, whom, by instinct, you salute, may you find our lot tempered by honor; unlike the Compromised whom by desire you commend, may you find my faith shielded by courage. The words and deeds of the Weak are all in the hands of the Absolute; you would have no power over them or me, if it were not first given.

You, all, I wait upon Him; to the union of His idea of

Love embodied in each, as attraction then content, by such harmonic accord with eternal Love as He has risen, so too will I; For risen He has, indeed it is true.

The Way of the Weak

Though there is limited space at my present disposal, by which I can only mimic the path, I wish to offer such respite as can be found in a devotion, born from our culture, and approved by custom; that the faithful Weak may enter into the path of justice by the way of mercy and hope.

* * *

Opening plea: Lord, we praise you and we thank you; we ask you to bless this small act of prayer, and to keep us ever mindful of those who do have not have as much as we do; be with everyone here, keep us all healthy and in your will; be with all our endeavors; and help us to enjoy the life you have given us.

Of our first parents

Psalm refrain: *Oh God, you are my God; for you my soul is thirsting; my body pines for you like dry, weary land without water; so I gaze on you in the sanctuary to see your strength and your glory; for your Love is better than life.*

In hope the Lord said: *It is not good that the man should be alone.*

In mercy you told us: *We shall not eat of the tree of knowledge of good and evil; in our frailty we did, and now rely on Your mercy;*

In justice you promised: *His head will be crushed. I will put enmity between you and the woman, and between your seed and her seed; he shall bruise your head, and you shall bruise his heel, in this promise lies our hope.*

We, the Weak, are no less complicit than our first parents; to this day we eat from the tree of knowledge of good and evil; yet, emboldened by our Friend, the Lord, in grace we crush the head, and no longer alone, by Him we are restored in justice.

Of our father Noah

Psalm refrain: *Oh God, you are my God; for you my soul is thirsting; my body pines for you like dry, weary land without water; so I gaze on you in the sanctuary to see your strength and your glory; for your Love is better than life.*

> In hope the Lord said: *Every moving thing that lives shall be food for you; and as I gave you the green plants, I give you everything;*

In mercy you told us: *Whoever sheds the blood of man, by man shall his blood be shed; for God made man in his own image.*

> In justice you promised: *When the bow is in the clouds, I will look upon it and remember the everlasting covenant between God and every living creature of all flesh that is upon the earth;*

We, the Weak, no less complicit than the people in the time of Noah, in our actions and in our hearts, we shed the blood of man, made in your image, but recalling the sign of your promise, by Him we are restored in justice.

Of our father Abraham

Psalm refrain: *Oh God, you are my God; for you my soul is thirsting; my body pines for you like dry, weary land without water; so I gaze on you in the sanctuary to see your strength and your glory; for your Love is better than life.*

In hope the Lord said: *I have chosen him, that he may charge his children and his household after him to keep the way of the Lord by doing righteousness and justice; so that the Lord may bring to Abraham what he has promised him;*

In mercy you told us: *Know of a surety that your descendants will be sojourners in a land that is not theirs, and will be slaves there, and they will be oppressed for four hundred years.*

In justice you promised: *I will establish my covenant between me and you and your descendants after you throughout their generations for an everlasting covenant, to be God to you and to your descendants after you;*

We, the Weak, no less complicit in not keeping the way of the Lord, but with trust that our deserved oppression is temporal, and that in your everlasting promise as given to all generations, by Him we are restored in justice.

Of our father Moses

Psalm refrain: *Oh God, you are my God; for you my soul is thirsting; my body pines for you like dry, weary land without water; so I gaze on you in the sanctuary to see your strength and your glory; for your Love is better than life.*

In hope the Lord said: *I am the God of your father, the God of Abraham, the God of Isaac, and the God of Jacob. And Moses hid his face, for he was afraid to look at God;*

In mercy you told us: Because you did not believe in me, to sanctify me in the eyes of the people of Israel, therefore you shall not bring this assembly into the land which I have given them.

In justice you promised: *Come up to me on the mountain, and wait there, and I will give you the tables of stone, with the law and the commandment, which I have written for their instruction.*

We, the Weak, are no less complicit, for in fear we hide our belief, rebelling from you our God, but on the mountain alone with you we are given the words of instruction, by Him we are restored in justice.

Of our father David

Psalm refrain: *Oh God, you are my God; for you my soul is thirsting; my body pines for you like dry, weary land without water; so I gaze on you in the sanctuary to see your strength and your glory; for your Love is better than life.*

In hope the Lord said: *I will make you a house. When your days are fulfilled and you lie down with your fathers, I will raise up your offspring after you, who shall come forth from your body, and I will establish his kingdom.*

In mercy you told us: *David arose from his couch and was walking upon the roof of the king's house, that he saw from the roof a woman bathing; and the woman was very beautiful; so David sent messengers, and took her; and she came to him, and he lay with her.*

In justice you promised: *David said to Nathan, I have sinned against the Lord. And Nathan said to David, The Lord also has put away your sin; you shall not die.*

We, the Weak, are no less complicit in turning away from you who redeem us, for we bring titillation and desire into our hearts, but in repentance you are quick to put away our sin, and by Him we are restored in justice.

Of our brother Mark

Psalm refrain: *Oh God, you are my God; for you my soul is thirsting; my body pines for you like dry, weary land without water; so I gaze on you in the sanctuary to see your strength and your glory; for your Love is better than life.*

> In hope the Lord said: *Behold, I send my messenger before thy face, who shall prepare thy way; the voice of one crying in the wilderness: Prepare the way of the Lord, make his paths straight.*

In mercy you told us: *If your eye causes you to sin, pluck it out; it is better for you to enter the kingdom of God with one eye than with two eyes to be thrown into Gehenna, where the worm does not die, and the fire is not quenched.*

> In justice you promised: *Even the dogs under the table eat the children's crumbs. And he said to her, for this saying you may go your way; the demon has left your daughter. And she went home, and found the child lying in bed, and the demon gone.*

We, the Weak, are no less complicit in seeing and hearing that which causes us to sin, but with undeserved scraps we are granted entrance to the kingdom, by Him we are restored in justice.

Of our brother Matthew

Psalm refrain: *Oh God, you are my God; for you my soul is thirsting; my body pines for you like dry, weary land without water; so I gaze on you in the sanctuary to see your strength and your glory; for your Love is better than life.*

In hope the Lord said: *Wise men from the East came to Jerusalem, saying, where is he who has been born king of the Jews? For we have seen his star in the East, and have come to worship him.*

In mercy you told us: *Those who are well have no need of a physician, but those who are sick. Go and learn what this means, I desire mercy, and not sacrifice. For I came not to call the righteous, but sinners.*

In justice you promised: *Go nowhere among the Gentiles, and enter no town of the Samaritans, but go rather to the lost sheep of the house of Israel. And preach as you go, saying, the kingdom of heaven is at hand.*

We, the Weak, are no less complicit in expecting to substitute our sacrifices for mercy to others, but to Israel first you brought forth the kingdom of heaven, by Him we are restored in justice.

Of our brother Luke

Psalm refrain: *Oh God, you are my God; for you my soul is thirsting; my body pines for you like dry, weary land without water; so I gaze on you in the sanctuary to see your strength and your glory; for your Love is better than life.*

In hope the Lord said: *Simeon blessed them and said to Mary his mother, behold, this child is set for the fall and rising of many in Israel, and for a sign that is spoken against, and a sword will pierce through your own soul also, that thoughts out of many hearts may be revealed.*

In mercy you told us: *No servant can serve two masters; for either he will hate the one and love the other, or he will be devoted to the one and despise the other. You cannot serve God and mammon. The Pharisees, who were lovers of money, heard all this, and they scoffed at him.*

In justice you promised: *I tell you, there will be more joy in heaven over one sinner who repents than over ninety-nine righteous persons who need no repentance;*

We, the Weak, are no less complicit in serving the master of plenty and scoff at reproach, but in a repentance of precarity like the lone sinner, by Him we are restored in justice.

Of our brother John

Psalm refrain: *Oh God, you are my God; for you my soul is thirsting; my body pines for you like dry, weary land without water; so I gaze on you in the sanctuary to see your strength and your glory; for your Love is better than life.*

In hope the Lord said: *In the beginning was the Word, and the Word was with God, and the Word was God. He was in the beginning with God.*

In mercy you told us: *When he heard that Jesus had come from Judea to Galilee, he went and begged him to come down and heal his son, for he was at the point of death. Jesus therefore said to him, unless you see signs and wonders you will not believe;*

In justice you promised: *While you have the light, believe in the light, that you may become sons of light.*

We, the Weak, are no less complicit by demanding signs and wonders to confirm our faith, but you as the light, have given us this light of love as Being, by Him we are restored in justice.

Of the return of our Friend

Psalm refrain: *Oh God, you are my God; for you my soul is thirsting; my body pines for you like dry, weary land without water; so I gaze on you in the sanctuary to see your strength and your glory; for your Love is better than life.*

> In hope the Lord said: *I am the Alpha and the Omega, says the Lord God, who is and who was and who is to come, the Almighty;*

In mercy you told us: *Because you are lukewarm, and neither cold nor hot, I will spew you out of my mouth. For you say, I am rich, I have prospered, and I need nothing; not knowing that you are wretched, pitiable, poor, blind, and naked.*

> In justice you promised: *Behold, the dwelling of God is with men. He will dwell with them, and they shall be his people, and God himself will be with them; he will wipe away every tear from their eyes, and death shall be no more, neither shall there be mourning nor crying nor pain any more, for the former things have passed away.*

We, the Weak, are no less complicit in our compromises and radical ambitions, but dwelling in us these errors will one day pass away, with tears and pains gone, by Him we are restored in justice.

* * *

Closing plea: *Lord, there is none like you; you created us in love and for love, sustain us by your Being. We ask only that you complete what you have begun in us; and with all of creation, rest not until by your Word we are in truth declared very good.*

About the Author

STEPHEN BUJNO, Ph.D., has endeavored to live an examined life, whether in the classroom, in literary form, or at the potter's wheel. As academic, he teaches philosophy and ethics for health care professionals at Villanova University. His published writings include *Ethics of Care and Wellness*; *Moral Being: Freedom, Society, and Beauty*; and *Autonomy, Consciousness, and Personhood*. As lifelong clay artist, he still assists his wife Tina in her studio. Married for thirty-six years, they are parents of three daughters, and grandparents of seven, all living and sharing close by in southwestern Pennsylvania.

www.ingramcontent.com/pod-product-compliance
Lightning Source LLC
LaVergne TN
LVHW090519110826
845146LV00003B/923